MASTER THE™ DSST®

Substance
Abuse
Exam

About Peterson's

Peterson's® has been your trusted educational publisher for over 50 years. It's a milestone we're quite proud of, as we continue to offer the most accurate, dependable, high-quality educational content in the field, providing you with everything you need to succeed. No matter where you are on your academic or professional path, you can rely on Peterson's for its books, online information, expert test-prep tools, the most up-to-date education exploration data, and the highest quality career success resources—everything you need to achieve your education goals. For our complete line of products, visit **www.petersons.com**.

For more information, contact Peterson's, 4380 S. Syracuse Street, Suite 200, Denver CO 80237; 800-338-3282 Ext. 54229; or find us online at **www.petersons.com**.

ISBN-13: 978-0-7689-4473-0

Printed in the United States of America

10 9 8 7 6 5 4 3 2 1   23   22   21

Contents

Before You Begin

HOW THIS BOOK IS ORGANIZED

Peterson's *Master the*™ *DSST*® *Introduction to World Religions Exam* provides a diagnostic test, subject-matter review, and a post-test.

- **Diagnostic Test**—Twenty multiple-choice questions, followed by an answer key with detailed answer explanations
- **Assessment Grid**—A chart designed to help you identify areas that you need to focus on based on your test results
- **Subject-Matter Review**—General overview of the exam subject, followed by a review of the relevant topics and terminology covered on the exam
- **Post-test**—Sixty multiple-choice questions, followed by an answer key and detailed answer explanations

The purpose of the diagnostic test is to help you figure out what you know—or don't know. The twenty multiple-choice questions are similar to the ones found on the DSST exam, and they should provide you with a good idea of what to expect. Once you take the diagnostic test, check your answers to see how you did. Included with each correct answer is a brief explanation regarding why a specific answer is correct, and in many cases, why other options are incorrect. Use the assessment grid to identify the questions you miss so that you can spend more time reviewing that information later. As with any exam, knowing your weak spots greatly improves your chances of success.

Following the diagnostic test is a subject-matter review. The review summarizes the various topics covered on the DSST exam. Key terms are defined; important concepts are explained; and when appropriate, examples are provided. As you read the review, some of the information may seem familiar while other information may seem foreign. Again, take note of the unfamiliar because that will most likely cause you problems on the actual exam.

After studying the subject-matter review, you should be ready for the post-test. The post-test contains sixty multiple-choice items, and it will serve as a dry run for the real DSST exam. There are complete answer explanations at the end of the test.

OTHER DSST® PRODUCTS BY PETERSON'S

Books, flashcards, practice tests, and videos available online at **www.petersons.com/testprep/dsst**

- A History of the Vietnam War
- Art of the Western World
- Astronomy
- Business Mathematics
- Business Ethics and Society
- Civil War and Reconstruction
- Computing and Information Technology
- Criminal Justice
- Environmental Science
- Ethics in America
- Ethics in Technology
- Foundations of Education
- Fundamentals of College Algebra
- Fundamentals of Counseling
- Fundamentals of Cybersecurity
- General Anthropology
- Health and Human Development
- History of the Soviet Union
- Human Resource Management

- Introduction to Business
- Introduction to Geography
- Introduction to Geology
- Introduction to Law Enforcement
- Introduction to World Religions
- Lifespan Developmental Psychology
- Math for Liberal Arts
- Management Information Systems
- Money and Banking
- Organizational Behavior
- Personal Finance
- Principles of Advanced English Composition
- Principles of Finance
- Principles of Public Speaking
- Principles of Statistics
- Principles of Supervision
- Substance Abuse
- Technical Writing

Like what you see? Get unlimited access to Peterson's full catalog of DSST practice tests, instructional videos, flashcards, and more for **75% off the first month!** Go to **www.petersons.com/testprep/dsst** and use coupon code **DSST2020** at checkout. Offer expires July 1, 2021.

Chapter 1

All About the DSST® Exam

WHAT IS DSST®?

Previously known as the DANTES Subject Standardized Tests, the DSST program provides the opportunity for individuals to earn college credit for what they have learned outside of the traditional classroom. Accepted or administered at more than 1,900 colleges and universities nationwide and approved by the American Council on Education (ACE), the DSST program enables individuals to use the knowledge they have acquired outside the classroom to accomplish their educational and professional goals.

WHY TAKE A DSST® EXAM?

DSST exams offer a way for you to save both time and money in your quest for a college education. Why enroll in a college course in a subject you already understand? For more than 30 years, the DSST program has offered the perfect solution for individuals who are knowledgeable in a specific subject and want to save both time and money. A passing score on a DSST exam provides physical evidence to universities of proficiency in a specific subject. More than 1,900 accredited and respected colleges and universities across the nation award undergraduate credit for passing scores on DSST exams. With the DSST program, individuals can shave months off the time it takes to earn a degree.

The DSST program offers numerous advantages for individuals in all stages of their educational development:

- Adult learners
- College students
- Military personnel

1

Adult learners desiring college degrees face unique circumstances—demanding work schedules, family responsibilities, and tight budgets. Yet adult learners also have years of valuable work experience that can frequently be applied toward a degree through the DSST program. For example, adult learners with on-the-job experience in business and management might be able to skip the Business 101 courses if they earn passing marks on DSST exams such as Introduction to Business and Principles of Supervision.

Adult learners can put their prior learning into action and move forward with more advanced course work. Adults who have never enrolled in a college course may feel a little uncertain about their abilities. If this describes your situation, then sign up for a DSST exam and see how you do. A passing score may be the boost you need to realize your dream of earning a degree. With family and work commitments, adult learners often feel they lack the time to attend college. The DSST program provides adult learners with the unique opportunity to work toward college degrees without the time constraints of semester-long course work. DSST exams take two hours or less to complete. In one weekend, you could earn credit for multiple college courses.

The DSST exams also benefit students who are already enrolled in a college or university. With college tuition costs on the rise, most students face financial challenges. The fee for each DSST exam starts at $85 (plus administration fees charged by some testing facilities)—significantly less than the $750 average cost of a 3-hour college class. Maximize tuition assistance by taking DSST exams for introductory or mandatory course work. Once you earn a passing score on a DSST exam, you are free to move on to higher-level course work in that subject matter, take desired electives, or focus on courses in a chosen major.

Not only do college students and adult learners profit from DSST exams, but military personnel reap the benefits as well. If you are a member of the armed services at home or abroad, you can initiate your post-military career by taking DSST exams in areas with which you have experience. Military personnel can gain credit anywhere in the world, thanks to the fact that almost all of the tests are available through the internet at designated testing locations. DSST testing facilities are located at more than 500 military installations, so service members on active duty can get a jump-start on a post-military career with the DSST program. As an additional incentive, DANTES (Defense Activity for Non-Traditional Education Support) provides funding for DSST test fees for eligible members of the military

More than 30 subject-matter tests are available in the fields of Business, Humanities, Math, Physical Science, Social Sciences, and Technology.

Available DSST® Exams

Business	Social Sciences
Business Ethics and Society	A History of the Vietnam War
Business Mathematics	Art of the Western World
Computing and Information Technology	Criminal Justice
Human Resource Management	Foundations of Education
Introduction to Business	Fundamentals of Counseling
Management Information Systems	General Anthropology
Money and Banking	History of the Soviet Union
Organizational Behavior	Introduction to Geography
Personal Finance	Introduction to Law Enforcement
Principles of Finance	Lifespan Developmental Psychology
Principles of Supervision	Substance Abuse
	The Civil War and Reconstruction

Humanities	Physical Sciences
Ethics in America	Astronomy
Introduction to World Religions	Environmental Science
Principles of Advanced English Composition	Health and Human Development
Principles of Public Speaking	Introduction to Geology

Math	Technology
Fundamentals of College Algebra	Ethics in Technology
Math for Liberal Arts	Fundamentals of Cybersecurity
Principles of Statistics	Technical Writing

As you can see from the table, the DSST program covers a wide variety of subjects. However, it is important to ask two questions before registering for a DSST exam.

1. Which universities or colleges award credit for passing DSST exams?
2. Which DSST exams are the most relevant to my desired degree and my experience?

Knowing which universities offer DSST credit is important. In all likelihood, a college in your area awards credit for DSST exams, but find out before taking an exam by contacting the university directly. Then review the list of DSST exams to determine which ones are most relevant to the degree you are seeking and to your base of knowledge. Schedule an appointment with your college adviser to determine which exams best fit your degree program and which college courses the DSST exams can replace. Advisers should also be able to tell you the minimum score required on the DSST exam to receive university credit.

DSST® TEST CENTERS

You can find DSST testing locations in community colleges and universities across the country. Check the DSST website (**www.getcollegecredit.com**) for a location near you or contact your local college or university to find out if the school administers DSST exams. Keep in mind that some universities and colleges administer DSST exams only to enrolled students. DSST testing is available to men and women in the armed services at more than 500 military installations around the world.

HOW TO REGISTER FOR A DSST® EXAM

Once you have located a nearby DSST testing facility, you need to contact the testing center to find out the exam administration schedule. Many centers are set up to administer tests via the internet, while others use printed materials. Almost all DSST exams are available as online tests, but the method used depends on the testing center. The cost for each DSST exam starts at $85, and many testing locations charge a fee to cover their costs for administering the tests. Credit cards are the only accepted payment method for taking online DSST exams. Credit card, certified check, and money order are acceptable payment methods for paper-and-pencil tests.

Test takers are allotted two score reports—one mailed to them and another mailed to a designated college or university, if requested. Online tests generate unofficial scores at the end of the test session, while individuals taking paper tests must wait four to six weeks for score reports.

PREPARING FOR A DSST® EXAM

Even though you are knowledgeable in a certain subject matter, you should still prepare for the test to ensure you achieve the highest score possible. The first step in studying for a DSST exam is to find out what will be on the specific test you have chosen. Information regarding test content is located on the DSST fact sheets, which can be downloaded at no cost from **www.getcollegecredit.com**. Each fact sheet outlines the topics covered on a subject-matter test, as well as the approximate percentage assigned to each topic. For example, questions on the Substance Abuse exam are distributed in the following way: Overview of Substance Abuse and Dependence—12%; Classification of Drugs—6%; Pharmacological and Neurophysiological Principles—6%; Alcohol—14%; Anti-Anxiety, Sedative, and Hypnotics—6%; Inhalants—6%; Tobacco and Nicotine—10%; Psychomotor Stimulants—6%; Opioids—8%; Cannabinoids—11%; Hallucinogens—4%; Other Drugs of Abuse—4%; Antipsychotic drugs—3%; and Antidepressants and Mood Stabilizers—4%.

In addition to the breakdown of topics on a DSST exam, the fact sheet also lists recommended reference materials. If you do not own the recommended books, then check college bookstores. Avoid paying high prices for new textbooks by looking online for used textbooks. Don't panic if you are unable to locate a specific textbook listed on the fact sheet; the textbooks are merely recommendations. Instead, search for comparable books used in university courses on the specific subject. Current editions are ideal, and it is a good idea to use at least two references when studying for a DSST exam. Of course, the subject matter provided in this book will be a sufficient review for most test takers. However, if you need additional information, it is a good idea to have some of the reference materials at your disposal when preparing for a DSST exam.

Fact sheets include other useful information in addition to a list of reference materials and topics. Each fact sheet includes subject-specific sample questions like those you will encounter on the DSST exam. The sample questions provide an idea of the types of questions you can expect on the exam. Test questions are multiple-choice with one correct answer and three incorrect choices.

The fact sheet also includes information about the number of credit hours ACE has recommended be awarded by colleges for a passing DSST exam score. However, you should keep in mind that not all universities and colleges adhere to the ACE recommendation for DSST credit hours. Some institutions require DSST exam scores higher than the minimum score recommended by ACE. Once you have acquired appropriate reference materials and you have the outline provided on the fact sheet, you are ready to start studying, which is where this book can help.

TEST DAY

After reviewing the material and taking practice tests, you are finally ready to take your DSST exam. Follow these tips for a successful test day experience.

1. **Arrive on time.** Not only is it courteous to arrive on time to the DSST testing facility, but it also allows plenty of time for you to take care of check-in procedures and settle into your surroundings.

2. **Bring identification.** DSST test facilities require that candidates bring a valid government-issued identification card with a current photo and signature. Acceptable forms of identification include a current driver's license, passport, military identification card, or state-issued identification card. Individuals who fail to bring proper identification to the DSST testing facility will not be allowed to take an exam.

3. **Bring the right supplies.** If your exam requires the use of a calculator, you may bring a calculator that meets the specifications. For paper-based exams, you may also bring No. 2 pencils with an eraser and black ballpoint pens. Regardless of the exam methodology, you are NOT allowed to bring reference or study materials, scratch paper, or electronics such as cell phones, personal handheld devices, cameras, alarm wrist watches, or tape recorders to the testing center.

4. **Take the test.** During the exam, take the time to read each question-and-answer option carefully. Eliminate the choices you know are incorrect to narrow the number of potential answers. If a question completely stumps you, take an educated guess and move on—remember that DSSTs are timed; you will have 2 hours to take the exam.

With the proper preparation, DSST exams will save you both time and money. So join the thousands of people who have already reaped the benefits of DSST exams and move closer than ever to your college degree.

SUBSTANCE ABUSE EXAM FACTS

The DSST® Substance Abuse exam consists of 100 multiple-choice questions that cover the history, effects, uses, administration, tolerance, withdrawal, overdose, prevention, and treatment of such substances as alcohol, anti-anxiety and sedative-hypnotic drugs, inhalants, tobacco and nicotine, psychomotor drugs, opioids, cannabinoids, hallucinogens, antipsychotics, antidepressants, and mood stabilizers. Careful reading, critical thinking, and logical analysis will be as important as your knowledge of substance abuse and treatment.

Area or Course Equivalent: Substance Abuse
Level: Upper-level baccalaureate
Amount of Credit: 3 Semester Hours
Minimum Score: 400
Source: https://www.getcollegecredit.com/wp-content/assets/
factsheets/SubstanceAbuse.pdf

I. Overview of Substance Abuse and Dependence – 12%

    a. Terminology

    b. Theories and models of abuse and dependence

    c. Demographics

    d. Costs to society and associations with social problems

    e. Screening and diagnosis

II. Classification of Drugs – 6%

    a. DEA schedule

    b. Pharmacologic effect

    c. Regulations

III. Pharmacological and Neurophysiological Principles – 6%

    a. Nervous system

    b. Actions of drugs

    c. Drug interactions

IV. Alcohol – 14%

    a. History and types

    b. Determinants of blood alcohol level

    c. Effects

    d. Uses and administration

    e. Tolerance, withdrawal, and overdose

    f. Dependency issues

    g. Prevention and treatment

V. Anti-Anxiety, Sedative, and Hypnotics – 6%

    a. History and types

    b. Effects

    c. Uses and administration

    d. Tolerance, withdrawal, and overdose

    e. Dependency issues

    f. Prevention and treatment

VI. Inhalants – 6%

    a. History and types

    b. Effects

    c. Tolerance, withdrawl, and overdose

    d. Dependency issues

    e. Prevention and treatment

    f. Uses and administration

VII. Tobacco and Nicotine – 10%

    a. History and types

    b. Effects

    c. Tolerance, withdrawal, and overdose

    d. Dependency issues

    e. Prevention and treatment

VIII. Psychomotor Stimulants – 6%

    a. History and types

    b. Effects

    c. Uses and administration

    d. Tolerance, withdrawal, and overdose

    e. Dependency issues

    f. Prevention and treatment

IX. Opioids – 8%

    a. History and types

    b. Effects

    c. Uses and administration

    d. Tolerance, withdrawal, and overdose

    e. Dependency issues

    f. Prevention and treatment

X. Cannabinoids – 11%

    a. History and types

    b. Effects

    c. Uses and administration

    d. Tolerance, withdrawal, and overdose

    e. Dependency issues

    f. Prevention and treatment

    g. Current trends

XI. Hallucinogens – 4%

    a. History and types

    b. Effects

    c. Uses and administration

    d. Tolerance, withdrawal, and overdose

XII. Other Drugs of Abuse – 4%

    a. Anabolic steroids

    b. Over-the-counter (OTC) substances

    c. Synthetic substances

    d. Club drugs

XIII. Antipsychotic Drugs – 3%

    a. History and types

    b. Effects

    c. Uses and administration

XIV. Antidepressants and Mood Stabilizers – 4%

    a. History and types

    b. Effects

    c. Uses and administration

    d. Tolerance and withdrawal

Chapter 2

Substance Abuse Diagnostic Test

DIAGNOSTIC TEST ANSWER SHEET

1. Ⓐ Ⓑ Ⓒ Ⓓ
2. Ⓐ Ⓑ Ⓒ Ⓓ
3. Ⓐ Ⓑ Ⓒ Ⓓ
4. Ⓐ Ⓑ Ⓒ Ⓓ
5. Ⓐ Ⓑ Ⓒ Ⓓ
6. Ⓐ Ⓑ Ⓒ Ⓓ
7. Ⓐ Ⓑ Ⓒ Ⓓ

8. Ⓐ Ⓑ Ⓒ Ⓓ
9. Ⓐ Ⓑ Ⓒ Ⓓ
10. Ⓐ Ⓑ Ⓒ Ⓓ
11. Ⓐ Ⓑ Ⓒ Ⓓ
12. Ⓐ Ⓑ Ⓒ Ⓓ
13. Ⓐ Ⓑ Ⓒ Ⓓ
14. Ⓐ Ⓑ Ⓒ Ⓓ

15. Ⓐ Ⓑ Ⓒ Ⓓ
16. Ⓐ Ⓑ Ⓒ Ⓓ
17. Ⓐ Ⓑ Ⓒ Ⓓ
18. Ⓐ Ⓑ Ⓒ Ⓓ
19. Ⓐ Ⓑ Ⓒ Ⓓ
20. Ⓐ Ⓑ Ⓒ Ⓓ

SUBSTANCE ABUSE DIAGNOSTIC TEST
24 minutes—20 questions

Directions: Carefully read each of the following 20 questions. Choose the best answer to each question and fill in the corresponding circle on the answer sheet. The Answer Key and Explanations can be found following this Diagnostic Test.

---

1. Smoke released into the air from a lighted cigarette is known as

   A. mainstream smoke.
   B. nicotine smoke.
   C. sidestream smoke.
   D. active smoke.

2. Alcohol and tobacco are considered

   A. opioids.
   B. OTC drugs.
   C. illicit drugs.
   D. gateway drugs.

3. In general, how would you calculate the length of time it will take an individual to metabolize the alcohol he or she drinks?

   A. Multiply the number of drinks by two hours each.
   B. Each drink takes about 30 minutes to metabolize.
   C. Beer and wine take about 30 minutes to metabolize, and hard alcohol takes about two hours to metabolize.
   D. Each drink takes about one hour to metabolize.

4. When an individual is in withdrawal from alcohol abuse, which of the following could occur in Stage 3?

   A. Insomnia
   B. Delusions
   C. Tremors
   D. Seizures

5. Dr. Sigmund Freud advocated cocaine usage to treat

    A. schizophrenia.
    B. hallucinations.
    C. depression.
    D. anxiety.

6. Which region of a neuron stores neurotransmitters?

    A. Presynaptic terminals
    B. Cell body
    C. Dendrites
    D. Axon

7. One of the most common side effects of low doses of opioids is

    A. diarrhea.
    B. headaches.
    C. alertness.
    D. constipation.

8. Sedative-hypnotics often come in the form of

    A. leaves.
    B. pills.
    C. liquid.
    D. nasal spray.

9. An individual takes substances that create an antagonistic interaction. What does this mean?

    A. The individual takes more than one substance in which one enhances the effects of another.
    B. The individual ingests a combination of drugs in which one activates the dormant properties of another.
    C. The individual ingests a combination of drugs in which one drug blocks the effects of another drug.
    D. The individual takes a combination of more than one substance in which one causes no effect based on the properties of the other.

10. Which of the following is the most common physiological effect of using marijuana?

    A. Decreased blood pressure
    B. Increased aggression
    C. Decreased appetite
    D. Increased heart rate

11. What of the following is a characteristic of antipsychotic drugs?

    A. They are highly addictive.
    B. They block the effects of other substances.
    C. They are most often obtained by prescription.
    D. Discontinued use will lead to severe withdrawal.

12. Cocaine is categorized as a

    A. stimulant.
    B. depressant.
    C. hallucinogen.
    D. psychotherapeutic.

13. A long-term effect known to be associated with extensive marijuana smoking is

    A. seizures.
    B. lung damage.
    C. mouth cancer.
    D. brain damage.

14. What is the alcohol content of an 80-proof bottle of whiskey?

    A. 20 percent
    B. 40 percent
    C. 80 percent
    D. 100 percent

15. Which of the following asserts that drug abuse is the result of a biological condition?

    A. Personality predisposition model
    B. Characterological model
    C. Disease model
    D. Moral model

16. Which of the following is another name for hallucinogens?

   A. Analgesics
   B. Cannabis
   C. Depressants
   D. Psychedelics

17. Which type of drug is abused by placing a bag over the head?

   A. Opioids
   B. Inhalants
   C. Nicotine
   D. Antipsychotics

18. MDMA, GHB, and Rohypnol are examples of

   A. club drugs.
   B. herbal drugs.
   C. antidepressants.
   D. anabolic steroids.

19. A drug that requires a written prescription and cannot be refilled by phone-in requests is classified under which DEA schedule?

   A. Schedule I
   B. Schedule II
   C. Schedule IV
   D. Schedule V

20. Prozac is the most popular

   A. anabolic steroid.
   B. antidepressant.
   C. antipsychotic.
   D. mood stabilizer.

ANSWER KEY AND EXPLANATIONS

1. C	5. C	9. C	13. B	17. B
2. D	6. A	10. D	14. B	18. A
3. D	7. D	11. C	15. C	19. B
4. B	8. B	12. A	16. D	20. B

1. **The correct answer is C.** Sidestream smoke refers to the smoke that is released into the air from the end of a lighted cigarette. Mainstream smoke (choice A) is the smoke that a smoker inhales directly from the mouthpiece of a cigarette. Sidestream smoke does contain high levels of nicotine, but nicotine smoke (choice B) is not the correct terminology. Active smoke (choice D) is the smoke intentionally inhaled.

2. **The correct answer is D.** Alcohol and tobacco are considered gateway drugs. Gateway drugs are typically used first by individuals who later move on to illicit drugs, such as heroin and cocaine. Choice A is incorrect because alcohol and tobacco are not derived from opium. Alcohol and tobacco are licit drugs, so choice C is incorrect. Over-the-counter (OTC) drugs (choice B) are medicines purchased without prescriptions, such as antihistamines and aspirin.

3. **The correct answer is D.** Each drink takes about one hour to metabolize, regardless of the type of alcohol. The drink would need to be the standard size used for calculation. If an individual has three drinks, it will take about three hours to metabolize.

4. **The correct answer is B.** Delusions are a symptom of withdrawal associated with Stage 3. Insomnia (choice A) and tremors (choice C) are associated with Stage 1. Seizures (choice D) are associated with Stage 4.

5. **The correct answer is C.** Freud recommended the use of cocaine in the treatment of depression. Physicians prescribed cocaine for a number of medical purposes until the Harrison Act of 1914 made it illegal to use or distribute cocaine.

6. **The correct answer is A.** The presynaptic terminals store neurotransmitters, which act as chemical messengers. The cell body (choice B) contains the nucleus, and the dendrites (choice C) are treelike branches that receive transmitter signals. The axon (choice D) conducts electrical signals.

7. **The correct answer is D.** Constipation is one of the most common side effects of opioids. Because of this side effect, opioids are used to treat severe diarrhea, so choice A is incorrect. Opioids relieve pain rather than cause pain, so choice B is incorrect. Opioids are not stimulants, so alertness (choice C) is not a side effect.

8. **The correct answer is B.** Sedative-hypnotics often come in the form of pills and are most widely dispensed as prescription drugs.

9. **The correct answer is C.** An antagonistic interaction occurs when one drug blocks the effect of another drug. A reaction does occur, which eliminates choices B and D. Choice A is indicative of a potentiating effect.

10. **The correct answer is D.** Marijuana increases the heart rate among almost all users. Choice A is incorrect because marijuana's effect on blood pressure varies from slight increases to no change among users. Aggression (choice B) is not a typical effect of marijuana because most people feel relaxed. The opposite of choice C is true. The appetite increases with marijuana use.

11. **The correct answer is C.** Antipsychotics are most often obtained by prescription. Antipsychotics are not addictive as choice A erroneously indicates. They enhance the effects of other drugs, so choice B is incorrect. Because they are not addictive, withdrawal symptoms would not be severe, so choice D is incorrect.

12. **The correct answer is A.** Cocaine is a stimulant that triggers excitement and paranoia among frequent users. Alcohol and sleeping pills are categorized as depressants, so choice B is incorrect. Hallucinogens (choice C) alter the perceptions of users, which is not an effect of cocaine usage. Psychotherapeutic drugs, such as Prozac, are used to treat patients with extensive mental problems, so choice D is incorrect.

13. **The correct answer is B.** Experts agree that long-term smoking of marijuana decreases pulmonary capabilities, causes chronic lung diseases, and raises the risk of lung cancer. Seizures (choice A) and mouth cancer (choice C) are not linked with smoking marijuana. Some people believe that marijuana causes brain damage, but there is no evidence to support this suspicion, so choice D is not the best answer.

14. **The correct answer is B.** The alcohol content of an 80-proof bottle of whiskey is 40 percent. Proof is double the alcohol percentage. The proof of a bottle of alcohol is printed on its label.

15. **The correct answer is C.** According to the disease model of dependency, people abuse drugs and alcohol because of biological conditions. Choices A and B suggest that people develop chemical dependencies because their personality traits are predisposed to doing so. The moral model (choice D) asserts that people make a choice to abuse drugs and alcohol.

16. **The correct answer is D.** Psychedelics are hallucinogens. Analgesics (choice A) refers to opioids, cannabis (choice B) refers to cannabinoids, and psychedelics (choice C) are a separate category of drugs called depressants.

17. **The correct answer is B.** Inhalants can be ingested by placing a bag over the head with the substance released in the bag so the individual can breathe it in.

18. **The correct answer is A.** MDMA, GHB, and Rohypnol are all examples of club drugs. Both GHB and Rohypnol have been used as date-rape drugs to incapacitate victims of sexual assaults. MDMA, also known as ecstasy, is used at raves and nightclubs to increase sensory experiences.

19. **The correct answer is B.** Schedule II drugs (such as hydrocodone) have a high risk for abuse and dependence and require a written prescription in order to be filled at a pharmacy. Schedule I drugs (choice A) are illicit drugs (such as heroin) and are not prescribed. Schedule IV drugs (choice C) have a low risk of dependence and can be refilled by a phone request. Schedule V drugs (choice D) are over-the-counter medications and do not require a prescription.

20. **The correct answer is B.** Prozac is the most commonly prescribed antidepressant. Prozac, Paxil, and Zoloft are selective reuptake inhibitors. SSRIs are antidepressants considered safer than MAOIs and tricyclics because they have fewer adverse side effects.

DIAGNOSTIC TEST ASSESSMENT GRID

Now that you've completed the diagnostic test and read through the answer explanations, you can use your results to target your studying. Find the question numbers from the diagnostic test that you answered incorrectly and highlight or circle them below. Then focus extra attention on the sections within Chapter 3 dealing with those topics.

Substance Abuse		
Content Area	Topic	Question #
Overview of Substance Abuse and Dependence Abuse	• Terminology • Theories and models of abuse and dependence • Demographics • Costs to society and associations with social problems • Screening and diagnosis	2, 15
Classification of Drugs	• DEA schedule • Pharmacologic effect • Regulations	19
Pharmacological and Neuropsychological Principles	• Nervous system • Actions of drugs • Drug interactions	6, 9
Alcohol	• History and types • Determinants of blood alcohol level • Effects • Uses and administration • Tolerance, withdrawal, and overdose • Dependency issues • Prevention and treatment	3, 4, 14

Content Area	Topic	Question
Anti-Anxiety, Sedativ, and Hypnotics	• History and types • Effects • Uses and administration • Tolerance, withdrawal, and overdose • Dependency issues • Prevention and treatment	8
Inhalants	• History and types • Effects • Tolerance, withdrawal, and overdose • Dependency issues • Prevention and treatment • Uses and administration	17
Tobacco and Nicotine	• History and types • Effects • Uses and administration • Tolerance, withdrawal, and overdose • Dependency issues • Prevention and treatment	1
Psychomotor Stimulants	• History and types • Effects • Uses and administration • Tolerance, withdrawal, and overdose • Dependency issues • Prevention and treatment	12
Opioids	• History and types • Effects • Uses and administration • Tolerance, withdrawal, and overdose • Dependency issues • Prevention and treatment	7
Cannabinoids	• History and types • Effects • Uses and administration • Tolerance, withdrawal, and overdose • Dependency issues • Prevention and treatment • Current Trends	10, 13

Content Area	Topic	Question
Hallucinogens	• History and types • Effects • Uses and administration • Tolerance, withdrawal, and overdose	16
Other Drugs of Abuse	• Anabolic steroids • Over-the-counter (OTC) substances • Synthetic substances • Club drugs	2, 18
Antipsychotic Drugs	• History and types • Effects • Uses and administration	11
Antidepressants and Mood Stabilizers	• History and types • Effects • Uses and administration • Tolerance and withdrawal	20

Chapter 3

Substance Abuse Subject Review

OVERVIEW

OVERVIEW OF SUBSTANCE ABUSE AND DEPENDENCE

For thousands of years, alcohol and drugs have been used in society for medicinal and recreational purposes. Evidence suggests that substance abuse plagued societies of the past just as it does modern societies. Before addressing the different types of drugs and their unique effects, it is important to understand the terms and theories associated with substance abuse.

Terminology

Drugs are natural or artificial substances that improve, obstruct, or alter the functions of the mind and body. The term **illicit drug** refers to substances that are illegal to possess, such as heroin and cocaine. In contrast, **licit drugs** are legal and include caffeine, alcohol, and nicotine. Licit drugs are available for purchase without a prescription and include over-the-counter (OTC) drugs such as aspirin, cold remedies, and antihistamines. Alcohol and nicotine are considered **gateway drugs** because most people who abuse illicit drugs first try liquor and/or cigarettes.

Illicit substance use often begins with experimental or recreational use that becomes routine and expected in some way. While the user might not yet feel physical and psychological pulls, there is a strong desire for continual use. This use does not yet cause problems, but it signals the start of a problem as the user begins a regular habit of use, or **habituation**.

Psychoactive drugs mainly affect the central nervous system, and they result in changes to consciousness, thought processes, and mood. Many psychoactive drugs are prescribed for physical and mental problems, but it is when such drugs are misused or abused that problems can occur. **Drug misuse** refers to using prescribed drugs in ways other than recommended by a physician, such as taking too many pills at one time. **Drug abuse** occurs when a substance, either prescribed or illicit, is used in a manner that causes social, occupational, psychological, or physical problems.

Although the terms **dependence** and **addiction** often describe the same condition, medical professionals typically prefer the term **dependency**. The common use of **addiction** to describe people's overindulgence in everything from gambling to chocolate makes *dependence* a better and more specific term in discussing drug use. **Drug dependency** occurs when an individual uses a drug so regularly that going without it is physically and psychologically difficult and results in withdrawal symptoms. Withdrawal symptoms frequently include nausea, anxiety, muscle spasms, and sweating but can vary with different substances.

The criteria used to determine levels of abuse and dependency include frequency of use—asking, "How often does the individual use the substance?" As use becomes more frequent, criteria move from habituation to abuse to dependence. Criteria also consider whether the drug was obtained through illegal means. Alcohol is legal for individuals who are 21 and over, but cocaine is illegal. Reasons for use also factor in, as some individuals might use alcohol to relax after, for instance, a stressful workday. However, others may need the substance to treat medical conditions or to prevent withdrawal symptoms, like the hand tremors related to alcohol dependency. Finally, the effects of the use are a factor. Some people exhibit symptoms of tolerance and withdrawal, which indicate a higher level of abuse and dependence.

Theories and Models of Abuse and Dependence

Experts have analyzed and described drug addiction over the years and have developed three theories of dependency: **biological**, **psychological**, and **sociological**. The **biological theory** proposes that substance abuse stems from physical characteristics related to genetics, brain dysfunction, and biomedical patterns. People with such traits experiment with drugs and then crave them. The **psychological theory** proposes that the mental and emotional status of an individual leads to substance abuse. The **sociological theory** proposes that social and environmental factors influence substance abuse. Several additional theories stem from the sociological theory:

- **Social learning theory** emphasizes that individuals learn drug use behaviors from society, family, and peers.
- **Social influence theories** claim that a person's daily social relationships are the cause of substance abuse.
- **Structural influence theories** assert that substance abuse occurs because of the organization of an individual's society, peer groups, and subculture.

Models of abuse and dependence include the **moral model**, which states that a person chooses to abuse drugs and alcohol. The **disease model** indicates that a person abuses drugs and alcohol because of a biological condition. The **characterological or personality predisposition model** proposes that a person is inclined to develop a chemical dependency because of certain personality traits. Although the moral model is generally considered outdated by the scientific community, many people maintain that lifestyle choices and immorality lead to drug dependency. Supporters of the disease model assert that dependency is a chronic disease that progresses with time and requires treatment and therapy. Recovery groups like Alcoholics Anonymous and Narcotics Anonymous adhere to the disease model. The fact that a number of people with chemical dependencies are also diagnosed with personality disorders supports the personality predisposition model. Consensus does not exist with regard to any of the dependency models or to the three theoretical explanations of drug dependency.

Demographics

Although drug abuse occurs in all areas of society, researchers have detected certain trends. Among American college students, approximately 70 percent drink alcohol and about 25 percent smoke cigarettes. A smaller number uses illicit drugs: 20 percent admit to smoking marijuana and 2 percent use cocaine. Based on race and ethnicity, Asians have the lowest percentage of illicit drug use, while Native Americans have the highest percentage. Substance abuse is also more common among men.

Researchers have also discovered that teens who use illicit drugs are more likely to know drug-abusing adults. The same adolescents typically associate with peers who use drugs, have academic difficulties, and believe their parents are not sources of support or encouragement. In general, experts believe that society, community, and family influence an individual's first use of drugs or alcohol. However, long-term usage is determined by an individual's experience with the drug. Once a person becomes truly dependent, social factors like laws, costs, and availability have very little bearing.

Costs to Society and Associations with Social Problems

Substance abuse is a costly habit to maintain. According to the National Institute on Drug Abuse, a drug abuser needs $100 every day to support a narcotics habit. Unfortunately, criminal activity is the primary source of funds for many drug abusers. Burglary and shoplifting are the crimes primarily associated with drug abusers in need of money, and many heroin abusers become involved in prostitution. Researchers have identified at least three correlations between drugs and crime:
- Drug users commit more crimes than individuals who don't use drugs.
- Violence is frequently associated with the use of narcotics, such as cocaine.
- Crimes are often committed while under the influence of drugs.

In addition to criminal activity, substance abuse affects the healthcare system. Diseases associated with intravenous drug use, such as hepatitis B and HIV, require expensive treatment. Automobile accidents, drug overdoses, and babies born with fetal alcohol syndrome require costly medical intervention as well. Substance abuse also affects productivity in the workplace. Unlike people who abuse drugs such as heroin and LSD, most alcoholics are able to hold jobs. However, alcoholics have a tendency to be late for work, have on-the-job accidents, and miss work. Many employers require employees to take drug screening tests and are making drug and alcohol assistance programs more available to employees with dependency issues.

Screening and Diagnosis

Substance abuse problems are often identified when an individual begins to get into trouble with family, at work, with the law, or with their finances. As trouble develops and use continues, it is often a sign that an individual has developed a diagnosable **substance abuse disorder**. Diagnosis and screening for this type of disorder is normally conducted in a clinical setting by someone who has formal training in substance abuse evaluation and treatment, often a substance abuse counselor. The evaluation itself often takes two to three hours as the counselor asks many questions designed to gain a complete picture of an individual's life. The **biopsychosocial approach** looks at biological factors, such as medical conditions; psychological factors, such as the presence of other mental health issues; and social factors, such as the environment and support system the individual has.

CLASSIFICATION OF DRUGS

Drug classification varies by the purpose of the drug. For example, a physician may categorize an amphetamine as a weight-control tool because of the drug's ability to suppress food consumption. However, law enforcement may refer to that same drug as a Schedule II controlled substance. The following table shows the major drug categories and provides examples of the types of drugs in each category.

Major Drug Categories	
Category	Examples
Stimulants	Cocaine, amphetamines, Ritalin, caffeine
Depressants	Alcohol, barbiturates, sleeping pills, inhalants
Hallucinogens	LSD, mescaline, Ecstasy, PCP
Opioids	Opium, morphine, codeine, heroin, methadone
Cannabis	Marijuana, THC, hashish
Nicotine	Cigarettes, chewing tobacco, cigars
Psychotherapeutics	Prozac, Haldol

DEA Schedule

The US Drug Enforcement Administration (DEA) has created a classification system placing drugs, substances, and the chemicals used to make drugs into five categories. Drugs are placed into these different categories based on the chemicals used to make the drugs, the drugs' acceptable medical use, and the drugs' potential for abuse and dependency. The drugs are divided into schedules based on the abuse and danger risks ranging from the most serious in Schedule I to drugs with lower potential for abuse in Schedule V.

DEA Controlled Substance Classification System			
Schedule	**Characteristics**	**Risk**	**Examples**
Schedule I	Drugs with no currently accepted medical use with a very high potential for severe psychological and physical dependence	Severe risk of abuse and dependence	Heroin, lysergic acid dithylamide (LSD), marijuana, 3,4-methyleneioxy-methamphetamine (Ecstasy), methaqualone, peyote
Schedule II	Dangerous drugs with high potential for severe psychological and physical dependence	High risk of abuse and dependence	Hydrocodone, cocaine, methamphetamine, methadone, oxycodone, fentanyl, Adderall, and Ritalin
Schedule III	Drugs with moderate-to-low potential for psychological and physical dependence	Moderate-to-low risk of abuse and dependence, but less than Schedule I and II drugs	Ketamine, anabolic steroids, testosterone, Tylenol with codeine
Schedule IV	Drugs with low potential for psychological and physical abuse and dependence	Low risk of dependence	Xanax, Soma, Darvon, Darvocet, Valium, Ambien, Tramadol

Schedule	Characteristics	Risk	Examples
Schedule V	Drugs with the lowest potential for psychological and physical abuse and dependence	Lowest risk of dependence of the Schedule drugs	Robitussin AC, Lomotil, Motofen, Lyrica, Parepectolin

Pharmacologic Effect

When drugs are ingested, they act to create a change in the function of certain cells within the body which, in turn, leads to changes in body function and behavior. This occurs as the drug interacts with the parts of the cell receptor. Some drugs exert stronger influences on the receptors than others, and more than one drug could affect the same receptor. For example, amphetamine and methamphetamine are both stimulants that would affect the same receptors, but methamphetamine would have a stronger effect on these receptors.

The concentration of the drug at the site of the action also plays a part in the effects of the drug on the central nervous system: the greater the concentration, the stronger the reaction. This is often described with a **dose-response curve**. The dose-response curve indicates the quantity, or dosage, of a drug that will cause a given response. The response could be all-or-none, such as death, or continuous, such as changes in blood pressure, respiration rate, etc., that increase with increases in the drug.

Some target cells are more sensitive to the effects of the drugs based on genetic factors and changes made to the cells by previous use of the drug. Continued use of the drug on the target cells often results in a loss of sensitivity, called **tolerance**. Tolerance occurs as an individual's body adapts to the presence of a given drug. As the body adapts, an individual must take more of the drug to create the same desired effects.

The adjustment to the presence of the drugs over time can also lead to dependence. **Physical dependence** occurs as the body adapts so completely to the presence of the drug that removal of the drug from the system causes physical symptoms ranging from headache and nausea to insomnia and even heart failure. The body creates a new "normal" that includes the drug. When the drug is removed, the body physically tries to compensate. Often the drug user will take the drug again in order to alleviate the painful symptoms, thus reinforcing the abuse of the drug.

Adjustment to the presence of the drug also leads to **psychological dependence** on the drug. Individuals who become dependent on the drug spend a lot of time fixating on the drug's effects and feel continuous cravings for the drug. This leads to impulsivity and compulsive use of the drug based on a perceived emotional and psychological need for it.

When taken in moderate doses, **stimulants**, such as caffeine, provide energy to users. However, powerful stimulants, such as cocaine, often trigger manic excitement and paranoia, which is why stimulants are referred to as "uppers." **Depressants**, known as "downers," have the opposite effect of stimulants on the body. Low to medium doses lead to relaxation, a loss of inhibition, slow reaction times, and uncoordinated movements. The regular use of depressants may cause hallucinations and restlessness.

As implied by the name, **hallucinogens** cause users to have hallucinations and experience a distorted reality. Often referred to as psychedelics, hallucinogens alter a user's perceptions, such as taste, smell, hearing, and vision. Higher amounts of hallucinogens are needed to achieve the same effects because tolerance for such drugs builds up quickly. **Opioids** are categorized as analgesics, painkillers, or narcotics. Low doses lead to a relaxed state, while higher doses may induce sleep. Unlike depressants that cause reckless behavior and slurred speech, opioids lead to users being in a stupor. Individuals who regularly take heroin, codeine, or morphine may become withdrawn. The most commonly used illegal drug in the United States is marijuana, which is also known as **cannabis**, as it is made from the crushed parts of the *Cannabis sativa* plant. The main psychoactive ingredient in marijuana is delta 9-tetrahydrocannabinol (THC), which generates the "high" experienced by users. **Nicotine**, which is considered a gateway drug, is extremely addictive and found in cigarettes, chewing tobacco, and cigars. Although nicotine is legal, delivery through smoking can cause heart and respiratory problems and cancer among some long-term users. Medical conditions associated with secondhand smoke have led to the creation of "smoke free" policies for buildings, businesses, and restaurants.

Psychiatrists and physicians often prescribe **psychotherapeutic drugs** to control mental problems in patients. Antipsychotics, such as haloperidol, are a type of psychotherapeutic drug that have a calming effect on patients and help control hallucinations. Antipsychotics are often prescribed to patients diagnosed with schizophrenia, mania, and delusional disorder. Antidepressants, such as Prozac, are psychotherapeutic drugs prescribed to patients with severe depression.

Regulations

In the United States, the FDA regulates pharmaceuticals and monitors said drugs for their purity, safety, and effectiveness. The FDA maintains a three-part regimen for testing new drugs with human subjects. Phase one delivers low doses to healthy humans on a volunteer basis to examine absorption and potential side effects. Phase two selects subjects who possess the condition the drug intends to treat. Phase three shifts to a larger testing population suffering from the drug's targeted condition. With success in each phase of the trials, the FDA then can weigh benefits of the drug against negative outcomes of the trials and decide whether the product is ready for public consumption.

While the FDA regulates the pharmaceutical industry, illicit substances have had a more complicated history of monitoring and regulation at the federal level. In 1914, the Harrison Act restricted access to opioids, requiring opioid seekers to have a prescription or receive administration from a physician. In 1922, the Jones-Miller Act dramatically increased penalties for dealing illicit drugs. This trend of prohibition increased over the ensuing decades, treating users largely as criminals rather than those in need of treatment. By 1928, approximately one third of all federal prisoners were serving time for drug-related offenses. The regulation of illicit substances was managed by the Narcotics Bureau of the Treasury Department, connecting narcotics (as the term became a catch-all for illicit substances rather than just opioids) to tax law and commerce rather than public health. The shifting demographics for users after World War II, the spectrum of substances being used, and the complexity of the existing law indicated the need for reform. In 1970, the Comprehensive Drug Abuse Prevention and Control Act scrapped previous laws and laid the groundwork for much of existing drug enforcement. Not only did the 1970 act direct more funds to public health measures—and give some authority to the Department of Health—but it also established the Justice Department's Drug Enforcement Agency. As seen in earlier sections, the DEA has schedules for controlled substances. In addition to indicating drug type and likelihood of abuse, these schedules also dictate availability, as seen in the following chart:

Regulated Availability of Controlled Substances	
Schedule	Regulation of Availability
Schedule I	Illegal for consumer distribution; for research use only in a controlled setting
Schedule II	Requires written prescription—no refills and no phone-in prescription; often requires drug testing in physician's office before a new prescription can be written
Schedule III	Requires prescription—written or oral; refills are legal without drug testing
Schedule IV	Requires prescription—written or oral; refills are legal without drug testing
Schedule V	Over the counter availability with proof of age

The regulation of availability would have a lasting impact on criminalization, punishment, and medical research (as discussed later in Cannabinoids: Current Trends). The years following the creation of the DEA saw various cultural changes and reactions that shifted the focus from public health back to criminality. Harsher penalties for illicit distribution and possession were enacted, and the Justice Department was given greater control over drug scheduling and thus regulation.

PHARMACOLOGICAL AND NEUROPHYSIOLOGICAL PRINCIPLES

Nervous System

The human body is constantly attempting to maintain internal stability, or **homeostasis**. Homeostatic mechanisms regulate body temperature, blood pressure, and glucose concentrations, as well as many other physiological functions. The human body works to maintain its internal stability to keep its organs and systems functioning properly, which is key to its survival. For example, a consistent body temperature of 98.6°F is optimal because a temperature that is too high or too low causes problems in certain parts of the body.

The nervous system plays a major role in body regulation. It sends messages to and from the brain, and these messages are influenced by outside agents that act on the components of the nervous system. The nervous system is composed of **neurons**, which are specialized nerve cells that transfer messages throughout the body. The human brain contains billions of neurons, which are all close to each other but never touch. All neurons consist of four regions:

1. *Cell body*: contains the nucleus
2. *Dendrites*: treelike branches that receive transmitter signals
3. *Axon*: long extension of the cell body that conducts electrical signal
4. *Presynaptic terminals*: store chemical messengers, which are known as **neurotransmitters**

Neurons communicate with each other by releasing neurotransmitters. These messengers are transmitted at a **synapse**. Synapses are the points of communication between neurons sending messages and neurons receiving messages. The small gap between one neuron and another is known as the **synaptic cleft.** Neurotransmitters travel across the synaptic cleft and bind to special proteins known as **receptors** on the outer membranes of target cells. The activation of receptors leads to a change in cell activity and is accomplished by both natural substances and drugs.

The nervous system is divided into the **somatic nervous system**, the **autonomic nervous system**, and the **central nervous system.** Neurons in the somatic nervous system are associated with voluntary actions, such as seeing, hearing, smelling, chewing, and moving one's arms and legs. The autonomic nervous system monitors involuntary actions, such as heart rate and blood pressure. The central nervous system consists of the brain and spinal cord and is responsible for learning, memory, and activity coordination.

The drugs in the major drug categories affect the central nervous system in order to produce a response that could ease negative physical effects of a health issue or treat a specific medical condition. As these drugs act to alleviate the pain or discomfort, they might also produce calming or euphoric effects that an individual may seek to continue to experience. In addition, some drugs are used to mimic or influence how the central nervous system responds, again creating euphoria and freedom from pain.

Actions of Drugs

Drugs have varying effects on the human body, including excitement, relaxation, and addiction. Analyzing how the nervous system works will lead to a better understanding of the variation in drug effects. As mentioned previously, neurotransmitters are chemical messengers released by neurons that have brief effects. Some drugs alter how neurotransmitters function. Certain neurotransmitters are associated with the introduction of psychoactive drugs into the nervous system, especially dopamine, acetylcholine, norepinephrine, serotonin, GABA, glutamate, and the endorphins. Many drugs that are abused, such as amphetamines and cocaine, alter dopamine neurons and cause paranoia, agitation, and euphoria. Serotonin is responsible for controlling mood, appetite, and aggressiveness, and substances such as LSD have been found to affect serotonin levels.

Different routes of administration have different effects. Drugs applied topically, such as ointment on the skin, tend to remain in the applied area. Transdermal application can be achieved by placing a patch on the skin with drugs that will release slowly from the patch over time. Oral administration involves placing the drug in the mouth and swallowing, which allows the stomach or small intestine to absorb it into the bloodstream. Drugs can also be administered sublingually by placing them under the tongue and allowing them to disintegrate in the mouth. Nasal administration involves spraying or applying the drug to the nasal cavities. Inhalation involves inhaling drugs that are in gas, liquid, or powder form. Drugs can also be injected with a needle and syringe. The injection can be subcutaneous, which injects the drug in liquid form into the subcutaneous tissue that lies just beneath the dermis of the skin. Intramuscular injection occurs in the muscular areas of the body. Intravenous injection administers the drug directly into a vein.

Drugs are metabolized, or processed, from an active form to a less active, potentially inactive, form. The principle organ of metabolism is the liver. Drugs administered orally are absorbed into the bloodstream via the stomach or intestines where they are immediately available for metabolizing by the liver before they create an effect on the target cells. Intravenous administration is often one of the most dangerous forms of administration because the drug avoids the absorption phase and potential partial inactivation by the liver.

Drug Interactions

Physicians prescribe medication to patients in order to treat an illness or relieve pain associated with a condition. In some cases, medication causes **side effects**, which are the unintended effects of a drug. Common side effects, such as nausea, vomiting, nervousness, breathing difficulties, dependence, and changes in cardiovascular activity, illustrate the fact that risks are associated with the consumption of any drug—over-the-counter, prescribed, and illicit. For example, morphine relieves pain, but it depresses breathing and causes constipation. Cocaine works well as a local anesthetic, but the drug's addictiveness outweighs its value in that capacity.

Both intended and unintended effects of a substance correspond to the amount consumed. **Potency** refers to the quantity of a drug that is required to produce an effect. In other words, a highly potent drug, such as LSD, requires a small dose to achieve a specific effect. **Toxicity** is a drug's capacity to harm the body, which may occur when any substance is taken in high doses. The consumption of extremely potent drugs, such as heroin, can cause serious damage to the body and possibly death. The presence of one drug can affect how another drug works in the body, a process known as drug interaction. Drug interactions are categorized into three types.

1. *Additive interaction*: Two drugs taken together equal the sum of the effects of each drug taken separately; occurs when both drugs are similar in structure (e.g., aspirin and acetaminophen).
2. *Antagonistic interaction*: One drug blocks the effect of another drug—also known as **inhibitory interaction**; this type of interaction is the basis for poison antidotes.
3. *Synergistic interaction*: The sum of the effects of two drugs taken together is greater than the effects of each drug taken separately (e.g., alcohol and acetaminophen).

Related to synergistic interactions are **potentiating effects**, in which one drug enhances the effect of another drug so that the combined effect is greater than the sum of the effects of each drug taken separately.

One of the most dangerous drug interactions involves any combination of depressants, alcohol, or narcotics. Since all three substances act in slowing down the breathing rate, a combination of any of them may result in one of the most common types of drug overdoses: respiratory depression. People who experience respiratory depression stop breathing and usually die without intervention. An example of an antagonistic interaction often initiated by drug abusers is the combination of alcohol and cocaine. The cocaine chemically combines with the ethyl alcohol in the body to create an extremely potent and toxic stimulant known as **cocaethylene**. Cocaethylene is suspected of causing a greater sense of euphoria than cocaine alone because it increases dopamine transmission.

ALCOHOL

As illustrated in the previous section, alcohol is dangerous when combined with other substances. However, consuming alcohol by itself also leads to problematic behavior, such as drunk driving, risky sexual behavior, and blackouts.

History and Types

Alcoholic beverages have been an aspect of society since ancient civilizations discovered fermentation, the chemical reaction that occurs when yeast converts sugar into alcohol. Mead, an alcoholic drink made from honey, was invented around 7000 BCE. Beer and berry wine were developed around 6400 BCE and grape wine in 300 BCE.

Distilled alcoholic beverages, such as brandy and whiskey, have alcohol concentrations greater than 15 percent. Distillation involves heating the mixture containing alcohol, collecting the vapors, and condensing the solution into a liquid once again. The process most likely originated in Asia around 800 CE. Today, **proof** indicates the alcohol content of a distilled beverage. Proof is twice the alcohol percentage, which means that a bottle of 100-proof vodka is 50 percent alcohol.

During the late eighteenth century, American citizens preferred alcoholic beverages to water partially because of water contamination issues. Much of society did not view alcohol negatively until after the Revolutionary War, when distilled spirits were associated with immoral and criminal activities. The heaviest period of alcohol consumption in the United States occurred between 1800 and 1808. The idea that people should avoid hard liquor, such as whiskey and vodka, and should only drink beer or wine in moderation was the basis of the **temperance movement** of the 1800s. The temperance movement eventually advocated complete abstinence from all alcoholic beverages. The Eighteenth Amendment to the US Constitution, enacted in 1920, prohibited the production, sale, and transportation of alcohol. However, Prohibition only pushed alcohol consumption underground.

People could purchase alcoholic drinks at illegal bars known as speakeasies, and bootleggers made and sold moonshine throughout the country. Prohibition was repealed in 1933 for a number of reasons: lost tax revenue, enforcement difficulties, black market liquor sales, police corruption, and political pressure.

Determinants of Blood Alcohol Level

The rate of alcohol absorption plays a significant role in **blood alcohol content (BAC)** level. Alcohol consumed on a full stomach is absorbed into the bloodstream slower than alcohol consumed on an empty stomach. Drinking water also slows the rate of alcohol absorption, while carbonated beverages increase it. Estimates of BAC levels are based on an individual's gender, weight, and alcohol consumption. Since alcohol does not dissolve into fatty tissues, a lean 200-pound man will have a lower BAC than a fat 200-pound man, all other variables being equal. Body weight is a significant factor as well. A 200-pound woman who drinks one beer will have a BAC of 0.022 percent, while a 100-pound woman who drinks the same amount will have a BAC of 0.045 percent. Blood alcohol content level is used as a measurement of intoxication and impairment for the legal and medical systems. A BAC level greater than 0.08 percent is illegal in every state in the United States. A BAC level of 0.4 percent to 0.6 percent is lethal because respiration is severely depressed. The following table shows the correlation between BAC and behavior.

BAC and Common Behaviors	
BAC Level	**Common Behavior**
0.05%	Reduced inhibition, decreased alertness, impaired judgment, relaxed mood
0.10%	Decreased reaction time, impaired motor skills
0.20%	Significant reduction in sensory and motor skills
0.25%	Staggering, severe motor skill disturbance
0.30%	Conscious but in a stupor
0.40%	Unconsciousness

Alcohol stays in the bloodstream until it has metabolized or been broken down by enzymes. More than 90 percent of alcohol metabolism takes place in the liver, which is why chronic drinkers often experience liver disorders, such as alcoholic hepatitis and cirrhosis. The liver metabolizes alcohol at a constant rate, no matter how much alcohol is consumed or the size of the person drinking. In general, the number of drinks consumed is the number of hours it takes a person to metabolize the alcohol.

Effects

Previous drinking experiences, mood, attitude, expectations, and circumstances are factors in an individual's behavior while drinking. However, when a person consumes alcohol, the effect of the alcohol depends mainly upon the amount of alcohol that is concentrated in the blood system. A person's blood alcohol content level determines how he or she behaves in response to alcohol consumption. In addition to liver diseases, heavy alcohol use is linked to the damage of almost every organ and bodily function. Alcohol affects the digestive system by irritating tissue and damaging the stomach lining. Neurological damage is apparent as many heavy drinkers suffer from irreversible impairment to memory and judgment.

Uses and Administration

Alcohol is a chemical group of compounds that includes ethanol, methanol, propanol, and pentanol. Alcohol is ingested orally in liquid form for recreational purposes. It is absorbed into the bloodstream quickly, based on the amount of food present in the stomach and the strength of the alcoholic drink. While ethanol is used to create alcoholic drinks used for recreation and relaxation, it is also used as a form of fossil fuel and can be diluted and distilled into perfumes. Further, ethanol is also used as a cleaning agent for general household cleaning and as a topical first-aid treatment for wounds.

Tolerance, Withdrawal, and Overdose

The socially acceptable nature of drinking lends itself to both psychological and physical dependency. The relaxing effect and positive feelings that occur with drinking make it routine for many people. The regular use of alcohol often leads to increased tolerance levels and decreased pharmacological effects, which may increase consumption and cause physical dependence. Alcoholics are individuals who are unable to function normally without consuming alcohol. Physical dependence becomes evident when alcohol consumption stops and withdrawal symptoms occur. Withdrawal effects from alcohol and barbiturates are more severe than effects associated with other substances. Withdrawal occurs in a progression of four stages:

Stage 1: tremors, restlessness, insomnia, rapid heartbeat, and heavy sweating

Stage 2: stage 1 symptoms plus hallucinations and vomiting

Stage 3: delusions, disorientation, and fever

Stage 4: life-threatening seizures

Dependency Issues

Dependency becomes a factor when an individual shows issues with use, continues to use, and becomes physically dependent on alcohol. If an individual ingests consistently larger quantities of alcohol for a period of time, the body will likely become dependent upon the substance. In the case of alcohol, body chemistry changes and withdrawal from a dependent state can become a serious medical concern. Individuals who decide to stop drinking after they have become dependent on alcohol are often weaned off the substance under medical supervision.

Prevention and Treatment

Once an individual has been diagnosed with an alcohol issue, the treatment process begins. First, there is an initial evaluation interview, after which a diagnosis is determined. Once the counselor has a diagnosis, the client and the counselor develop a treatment plan, which outlines the issues they will work on for a treatment period, usually 90 days. For chronic users who cannot stop without medical intervention, there are medications that, when taken, can create a negative reaction when alcohol is ingested. These medications create a negative physical and psychological association with alcohol. In general, treatment seeks to establish the reasons for the use, help the client stop using, and set up methods to maintain sobriety. These methods include attending twelve-step programs that provide peer support and attending individual and group counseling sessions.

Recovering alcoholics often face a more difficult journey than those who are dependent on other drugs, such as cocaine or heroin, because society generally finds drinking acceptable. Alcoholics Anonymous encourages addicts to stay connected with other alcoholics by attending chapter meetings and avoiding the social isolation that can trigger a relapse. Some alcoholics seek help from residential treatment centers for one or two months to avoid relapses.

ANTI-ANXIETY, SEDATIVE, AND HYPNOTICS

Sedative-hypnotics, also known as **central nervous system (CNS) depressants**, are frequently abused substances because of their ability to reduce CNS activity, decrease the brain's level of awareness, and relieve anxiety. Within the category of CNS depressants, sedatives relieve anxiety and fear, while hypnotics induce drowsiness and sleep.

History and Types

Prior to the development of CNS depressants, alcohol was commonly used to treat anxiety and nervousness. In the 1800s, **bromides** were introduced to induce sleep, but they were later found to be highly toxic. In the early part of the twentieth century, **barbiturates** such as phenobarbital replaced bromides as an anti-anxiety medication. However, scientists and physicians noticed a number of problems associated with barbiturates—tolerance, dependence, and respiratory depression. While many people safely took barbiturate sleeping pills, the medical community sought a better drug for the treatment of anxiety and sleep disorders.

During the 1950s, **benzodiazepines** were marketed as CNS depressants that offered a safe alternative to barbiturates. Benzodiazepines remain the most popular and safest CNS depressants prescribed by doctors today and include brand-name pharmaceuticals such as Valium, Ambien, and Xanax. Benzodiazepines are prescribed for the treatment of anxiety, neurosis, muscle tension, lower back pain, and insomnia. Like barbiturates, benzodiazepines increase the actions of the neurotransmitter GABA. **GABA** is the primary inhibitory neurotransmitter in the central nervous system and acts as the body's tranquilizer by inducing sleep and promoting calmness.

Effects

Small amounts of these drugs can relax muscles and calm the nervous system, easing symptoms of chronic anxiety or insomnia. Larger doses can reduce alertness, impair reflexes, cause irritability, and slur speech. Problems associated with barbiturates and benzodiazepines occur when they interact with other depressants, such as alcohol. Combining benzodiazepines with illicit drugs, such as heroin and cocaine, is common among substance abusers. Both barbiturates and benzodiazepines can cause physical and psychological dependence. Women who take these drugs during pregnancy can create dependency in their unborn children. Barbiturate overdoses can lead to suicide and accidental drug poisoning. Reduction of benzodiazepine use should occur over time in order to minimize withdrawal symptoms and avoid complications.

Uses and Administration

Anti-anxiety drugs and sedative-hypnotics are most often abused as prescription drugs. An individual either convinces the doctor of a need for the drugs and sells them to others or uses and abuses their own prescription. In most cases, these drugs are in pill form and are available as prescription pharmaceuticals, which means there is a higher level of regulation related to their distribution. Many of the drugs in this category are distributed legally as prescription drugs. Unfortunately, there is a common and erroneous belief that prescription drugs are safer than illicit drugs. As anti-anxiety drugs operate on the neurotransmitter GABA, which regulates a sedative effect, overdosing poses serious risks.

Tolerance, Withdrawal, and Overdose

Use of barbiturates and benzodiazepines over an extended period of time can result in tolerance, meaning that individuals who take them need to take increasingly more of the substance in order to experience the same effects. When the individual attempts to stop the use after a period of time, he or she would likely experience physical symptoms of withdrawal, including restlessness, insomnia, and potentially convulsions and death. Some individuals experience hallucinations, seizures, disturbed heart rhythm, and vomiting. Behaviorally, individuals might take less time with personal hygiene, experience psychomotor agitation and exhibit irritability and inability to focus. Individuals are often disoriented and have trouble determining person, place, and time when asked. There is reduced memory function and disorganization. Withdrawal effects can last as long as three weeks after the drug is no longer ingested. Individuals might experience increased sleeplessness and anxiety. Overdoses of these substances are often lethal, as nearly one-third of all reported drug-related deaths involve barbiturates and benzodiazepines.

Dependency Issues

Drugs in this class can create a pattern of behaviors that result in psychological and physical dependence. In the case of benzodiazepines, individuals find it hard to sleep without the drugs, and they become dependent upon them. Since quick cessation of benzodiazepine use can result in severe physical withdrawal symptoms, it is important to wean from them under the supervision of a physician, while also attending mental-health counseling.

Prevention and Treatment

In many cases, use of this category of drugs is related to stress and/or anxiety management. Many individuals start use as a prescription treatment for symptoms of anxiety and develop a psychological and physical dependence on the drugs. Treatment must address all aspects of the drug use and will include counseling and other behavior therapies. In this case, it is important to treat the issues that brought about the need to use and abuse anti-anxiety medications initially.

INHALANTS

Many everyday products normally found in a home have volatile ingredients that can cause psychoactive reactions when inhaled. While they are abused mainly by younger populations of children and adolescents, they are also abused by adults.

History and Types

Gasoline, paint, glue, air freshener, and nail polish are volatile substances that elicit euphoric feelings when inhaled. Although inhalant abuse may seem to be a modern trend, it actually dates back to the eighteenth century, when people inhaled nitrous oxide to attain a state of drunkenness. Inhaling nitrous oxide, or laughing gas, for recreational purposes continued for many years, and the inhalant is still used for some medical procedures such as dental work. During the 1950s, the public was made aware of teenagers becoming "high" by sniffing glue. Currently, teenagers and adolescents misuse over a thousand different products as inhalants. There are three categories of inhalants: **gaseous anesthetics**, **nitrites**, and **volatile solvents**.

Inhalants	
Category	**Examples**
Gaseous anesthetics	Nitrous oxide ("laughing gas"), ether, chloroform
Nitrites	Amyl nitrite ("poppers")
Volatile substances	Aerosols, toluene, butane, propane, gasoline, Freon

As previously mentioned, nitrous oxide is safe to use as a light anesthetic for outpatient procedures performed by dentists and physicians. Its availability in the medical community has led to its abuse by medical professionals who have access to it. The colorless gas is found in large balloons and in cartridges called **whippets** that are included in containers of whipping cream. Both are sources for inhalant abusers.

Nitrites are chemicals that cause a rapid dilation of the arteries combined with a reduction in blood pressure to the brain. The result of this vasodilation is a short feeling of faintness and sometimes unconsciousness. Nitrites were sold in small vials over the counter in the 1960s and were "popped" between the fingers and held under the nose for inhalation. Nitrites have not been available to consumers since the early 1990s.

The most prevalent category of inhalants is volatile substances. The easy availability and low cost associated with volatile substances makes them especially appealing to children and teenagers. Some states have passed laws to limit the sale of volatile solvents to young people, but, with so many kinds on the market, the effect has been minimal.

Types of Volatile Substances

Substance Type	Sources and Hazards
Aerosols	High concentration of chemicals from spray paint and other spray cans
Toluene	Chemical found in glues, paints, and nail polish; quickly absorbed by the lungs, brain, heart, and liver
Butane and propane	Highly flammable, especially when combined with smoking; found in lighter fluid
Gasoline	Widely available and highly flammable
Freon	Found in refrigerators, airbrushes, and air conditioners; danger of freeze injuries

Uses and Administration

Methods of inhalation vary. **Sniffing** or **snorting** refers to inhaling vapors straight from the product's original container. **Huffing** refers to soaking rags in a solvent and holding the rag over one's mouth. If highly concentrated substances are inhaled directly, it can lead to heart failure and death. **Bagging** is the term used to describe inhaling solvents that have been placed in paper or plastic bags. The high from inhaling lasts only a few minutes, which often means the individual inhales repeatedly over the course of a short period of time.

Effects

The initial effects of inhaling volatile chemicals are nausea, coughing, and sneezing. Low doses generate feelings of lightheadedness, disorientation, mild stimulation, and dizziness. High doses act like CNS depressants by producing relaxation, sleep, slurred speech, and possibly coma. Hypoxia (oxygen deficiency), brain damage, suffocation, and death may occur in some cases. In addition to the short-term health effects of inhalant abuse, users may experience permanent damage. Although teenagers who abuse inhalants typically move on to other drugs or alcohol, the damage of inhalant abuse is permanent. The inhalation of high concentrations of household products that contain multiple chemicals damages vital organs that absorb the inhaled substances. In addition, young abusers of inhalants are still growing and developing, and the toxic nature of inhalants may interfere with their mental development.

Tolerance, Withdrawal, and Overdose

Addiction to inhalants is not common but can arise with repeated use. Since the high is of such short duration, individuals often inhale numerous times over a short period. This can lead to overdose. Repeated use over longer periods of time can lead to symptoms of tolerance. Mild withdrawal can occur with long-term inhalant use over periods of many days.

Dependency Issues

Prolonged heavy use of inhalants could lead to dependency issues, although it is not common. More common is graduation to stronger substances that do have a higher addiction and dependence risk. The aftereffects are not long lasting but can be lethal without warning.

Prevention and Treatment

Since the population associated with inhalant use is younger, efforts to prevent this behavior often begin in school with information sessions. Students identified as at-risk will be given additional counseling and information. Parents can be included in the process so that they know what to look for at home. Since most products used for inhalation are found in the home, it is important for adults to understand the signs and consequences of even a single huff.

TOBACCO AND NICOTINE

Despite the fact that tobacco contributes to deaths related to cardiovascular disease and cancer, smoking remains a habit for nearly 17 percent of the US population aged 18 years or older (approximately 40 million adults). The deadly addiction is unlikely to cease anytime soon because each day in America almost 4,000 teenagers and young adults try smoking for the first time. Tobacco will likely remain part of America's future just as it has been part of America's past.

History and Types

The indigenous people of the New World introduced Christopher Columbus to tobacco in 1492, but native populations in North and South America had likely been smoking tobacco leaves for centuries. Explorers brought tobacco back to Europe, where it was initially viewed as an oddity. However, its use soon became popular. Europeans used tobacco leaves to treat over thirty different medical conditions, including headaches and abscesses. Some Europeans, such as King James I, believed that tobacco was evil because of its association with Native American religion and magic. He attempted to curb the use of tobacco by raising the import tax on it, but tobacco continued to be popular. Across the Atlantic, the tobacco industry flourished in Virginia and became a significant export of the American colonies.

Until the late nineteenth century, pipes, chewing, and snuff were the most popular methods of using tobacco, although some people enjoyed smoking cigars. The invention of a cigarette-rolling machine in the 1880s gave rise to the cigarette industry and forever changed the way people used tobacco. In 1885, American tobacco companies sold 1 billion cigarettes. Sales continued to rise over the years, reaching 702 billion cigarettes in 1992. Although American demand for cigarettes has dropped, more than 249 billion cigarettes were sold in the United States in 2017.

Effects

Nicotine entering the central nervous system triggers the release of the neurotransmitter **dopamine**, which causes feelings of pleasure. Within ten seconds of smoking a cigarette, nicotine reaches the brain, which may partially explain the abuse potential. Nicotine affects the body in a number of other ways as well, including:

- Decreasing the ability of blood to carry oxygen
- Increasing blood pressure, heart rate, and blood flow
- Diminishing the desire to eat for a short time

Although cigarette smoking has declined over the last twenty years (with as many as 45 million smoking adults in 2005), more than 34 million adults smoke cigarettes on a regular basis. One out of every five deaths that occurs in the United States can be traced to smoking—a preventable cause of death. Lung cancer, heart disease, stroke, and chronic lung disease are some of the specific causes of death for smokers.

The leading cause of death in the United States is cardiovascular disease, and research suggests that smoking increases a person's risk of having a heart attack. Fat deposits block the arteries of smokers and prevent blood from reaching the heart. However, the damage is not necessarily permanent. Studies have shown that people who stop smoking are able to lower their risk of heart disease over time.

Cancer is the second leading cause of death in the United States, and the risk of cancer increases with three factors:

1. Number of cigarettes smoked daily
2. Number of years spent smoking
3. Age at which smoking began

Although lung cancer is not highly common, it can be directly linked to smoking in approximately 85 percent of all cases. Cancers of the mouth, larynx, and esophagus are associated with smoking cigars and pipes. Like heart disease, cancer risks drop when smoking ceases, although it may take many years to reach the same risk level as nonsmokers. Lung ailments such as pulmonary emphysema, chronic bronchitis, and respiratory infections are more common among smokers than among nonsmokers.

The adverse health effects of tobacco are not limited to smokers. **Passive smoking** refers to the inhalation of cigarette smoke in the environment by nonsmokers. The smoker draws **mainstream smoke** directly from the mouthpiece of a cigarette. In contrast, **sidestream smoke**, which is also known as **secondhand smoke**, is the smoke that comes from the lighted end of a cigarette. Sidestream smoke pollutes the air breathed by both smokers and nonsmokers, and it contains high concentrations of carbon monoxide, nicotine, and ammonia. In conditions of limited ventilation and heavy smoking, sidestream smoke is responsible for numerous respiratory tract infections among children each year.

Most people are aware that cigarette smoking during pregnancy can be detrimental to a developing fetus. Women who smoke during pregnancy have a higher risk of a stillbirth and premature delivery. Babies of smokers usually have below-average weight and length because nicotine and carbon monoxide reduce the amount of oxygen and nutrients that flow to the placenta.

Uses and Administration

Tobacco is often ingested through cigarette smoking. Individuals inhale the substance through the cigarette, either filtered or unfiltered. Other individuals use smokeless tobacco that comes in the forms of chewing tobacco and snuff. **Chewing tobacco** is placed between the gum and teeth and absorbed through the saliva and bloodstream. **Snuff** can be used by sniffing or inhaling the tobacco into the nose. Individuals can also use **pipes** to smoke the tobacco. Pipes are reusable and the tobacco is placed in a bowl at the end of a stem. The other end of the stem contains the mouthpiece through which the smoke is drawn. **E-cigarettes** are battery operated electronic devices that are designed to produce a flavored nicotine vapor similar to tobacco smoke. The user puffs on it like they would a cigarette, which releases a vaporized solution of chemicals. Although they have been marketed as safe, they contain many known carcinogens and toxic chemicals. A **hookah** is a pipe used to smoke a combination of produce and tobacco, called a **Shisha**, which is heated. The smoke created by the heating is filtered through water. The filtration with water does not reduce the ingestion of toxic chemicals, and hookah smoking has been associated with many negative health risks. A new form of administration is **dissolvable tobacco**, which comes in the form of strips, sticks, or lozenges. They are free of smoke and snuff and are dissolved on the tongue or in the mouth like a breath mint or hard candy.

Tolerance, Withdrawal, and Overdose

As the nicotine is absorbed into the bloodstream, it immediately stimulates the adrenal glands to produce epinephrine, which stimulates the central nervous system. It also increases the activation of the neurotransmitter dopamine, which influences brain pathways that elicit reward and pleasure. After a period of time, these effects alter brain chemistry, causing the brain to need ever-increasing doses to produce the same effect. This causes tolerance. When an individual ceases tobacco use after a period of time, they often experience withdrawal symptoms, including irritability, sleep disturbances, and strong tobacco cravings. While there is no direct over-dose potential, the more individuals smoke, the more they increase their risk of heart disease, stroke, cancer, and many other terminal health issues.

Dependency Issues

The nicotine in cigarettes is highly addictive, which makes stopping the habit extremely difficult. Nicotine gum, nicotine skin patches, self-help classes, and counseling are all methods commonly employed to help smokers stop lighting up. Regular smokers who stop smoking without the use of cessation aids typically experience withdrawal symptoms, including irritability, insomnia, anxiety, poor judgment, and tobacco cravings. In some cases, signs of withdrawal may appear only a few hours after quitting and may last for months. Studies indicate that smoking cessation should be gradual rather than sudden, in order to avoid a relapse. Many smokers admit to a desire to quit, but most who try to quit on their own relapse within one week.

Prevention and Treatment

Nicotine is only one of over 4,000 chemicals in tobacco smoke, but it is the key to dependency. Nicotine is a colorless, volatile liquid alkaloid that is highly addictive. When a person smokes a cigarette, the nicotine is absorbed into the bloodstream. Nicotine activates the reward pathways through the increased release of dopamine. The effects peak within 10 seconds of inhalation and dissipate quickly, which encourages the need to continue smoking in order to maintain the pleasant feelings. A smoker experiences long-term brain changes with continued use of nicotine, which results in the addiction and dependency issues.

PSYCHOMOTOR STIMULANTS

Stimulants are substances that increase energy levels and generate a euphoric state for users. Cocaine and amphetamines are stimulants. Xanthine and caffeine, a type of xanthine, are stimulants often contained in foods and beverages such as chocolate, coffee, tea, and soft drinks. We will discuss each of these stimulants separately in the next few sections.[1]

---

1. Carteret Community College (n.d.). Xanthines. Retrieved from: http://web.carteret.edu/keoughp/
   LFreshwater/PHARM/ NOTES/Xanthines.htm

History and Types

Cocaine

Cocaine comes from the coca plant that grows in the Andes Mountains in South America. Citizens of the Inca Empire in Peru chewed coca leaves to provide relief from fatigue and to boost endurance for carrying loads over mountains. Coca leaves were used as currency at the time of the Spanish invasion in the sixteenth century. During the nineteenth century, French chemist Angelo Mariani used extractions from the coca leaf in a number of products, such as cough drops, tea, and wine. Mariani's cocaine extract was advertised as a magical drug that would lift the spirits and end fatigue. The chemist even received a medal of appreciation from the Pope for Vin Mariani, a red wine created with cocaine extract. In the 1880s, Dr. W. S. Halsted, an American physician, experimented with cocaine as a local anesthetic. Dr. Sigmund Freud also advocated the use of cocaine to treat depression and morphine dependence. Most physicians, however, realized that frequent recreational use of cocaine was dangerous, and the Harrison Act was enacted in 1914 to regulate use and distribution of the substance.[2]

Amphetamines

Patented in 1932, **amphetamines** were initially used for the treatment of asthma because of their ability to dilate bronchial passages. People soon realized that the over-the-counter amphetamine inhaler allowed users to stay awake for extended periods. During World War II, German, British, and Japanese soldiers used amphetamines to counteract fatigue, and US soldiers used it for the same reason during the Korean War.

In the 1960s, intravenous abuse of amphetamines began because the drug offered effects similar to cocaine when injected with heroin. At the time, doctors prescribed amphetamines for depression and obesity, so legal acquisition of the drugs was not an issue. Currently, **methamphetamines**, which are similar in structure to amphetamines and highly addictive, are rising in popularity among drug users. Methamphetamines offer longer-lasting effects than cocaine, and they can be made very easily and inexpensively in home laboratories.

----

2. National Institute on Drug Abuse (n.d.) Drugfacts: Cocaine. Retrieved from: https://www.drugabuse.gov/publications/drugfacts/cocaine

Xanthines

Xanthine is a type of purine that is produced by all human cells and by some plants and animals. Caffeine is one of the main types of xanthines and can be found in many food and drink products. Any food, drink, or medication containing caffeine contains xanthines.

The various types of xanthines include caffeine, theobromine, theophylline, and paraxanthine. Caffeine, theophylline, and theobromine can all be found in yerba mate and kola. Caffeine and theophylline can also be found in tea, while theobromine can be found in cacao. Paraxanthine is found in animals that have consumed caffeine. Xanthines are a group of alkaloids that are used as mild stimulants in treatment of certain respiratory issues.[3]

Caffeine is a chemical believed to be in use as a stimulant in one form or another since the year 850. In the time of explorations by Columbus, cocoa beans were used as money in Central America, or New Spain as it was termed at the time. In the early 1600s, coffee was introduced to Europe and its introduction as a mainstay in society was cemented. Since that time caffeinated drinks in various forms have become a regular item on the daily menus of many families. Although caffeine poses less of a risk than cocaine and amphetamines, heavy use can cause health problems. It is considered the world's most widely used psychoactive drug, and it is legal.

Effects

Cocaine

Cocaine is a highly addictive substance that produces short-term euphoria, energy, talkativeness, and dangerous increases in heart rate and blood pressure. It stimulates the central nervous system and increases the levels of dopamine, which regulate reward and pleasure. Cocaine can decrease appetite while increasing body temperature. Blood vessels constrict and pupils dilate as a result of use. Additionally, judgment is often impaired, leading to adverse behaviors.

----

3. Carteret Community College (n.d.). Xanthines. Retrieved from: http://web.carteret.edu/keoughp/ LFreshwater/PHARM/NOTES/Xanthines.htm

Amphetamines

In addition to alertness, amphetamines cause arousal and activate the fight-or-flight response in users. Effects associated with low doses of amphetamines include increased heart rate, blood pressure, and breathing, as well as decreased appetite. High doses may lead to convulsions, fever, and chest pain. Heavy amphetamine usage has also been associated with behavioral stereotypy, which is the meaningless repetition of a simple activity, such as repeating a word or cleaning an object. Chronic amphetamine usage damages brain cells and reduces the number of dopamine and serotonin neurotransmitters and can result in cardiovascular issues.

Xanthines

Caffeine increases energy utilization and efficiency in neurotransmissions involved in the cerebral cortex, which provides heightened alertness, concentration, and neuromuscular coordination. Caffeine can also be used to increase mood. Caffeine can produce negative side effects. Larger doses of caffeine can produce moodiness, anxiety, jitters, headaches, and fatigue. It has also been thought by some to be a gateway drug to other stronger substances.

Uses and Administration

Cocaine

In the early 1980s, cocaine was perceived as a safe and glamorous drug used by the wealthy and the famous. Its cost was too high for most people, until drug dealers in 1985 began selling crack, an inexpensive variety of freebase cocaine smoked in a glass water pipe. **Freebasing** is a method of reducing the impurities in cocaine to prepare the drug for smoking. The method by which cocaine is administered affects the drug's intensity, abuse potential, and toxicity level.

Methods of Using Cocaine	
Method	Effects/Abuse Potential
Chewing coca leaves	Least potent method; not likely to cause dependence or health issues; uncommon in United States

Method	Effects/Abuse Potential
Intravenous	Delivers high amount of cocaine quickly to the brain; intense "high" that lasts up to 20 minutes followed by "crashing"; dependency likely
Smoking crack cocaine (freebasing)	Similar effects to intravenous usage but more intense; preferred by some users over intravenous because no needles required; most addictive method
Intranasal (snorting cocaine powder)	Quick stimulation of CNS that lasts up to 40 minutes and is followed by "crashing"; most common administration method for recreational users

Amphetamines

Amphetamines were once prescribed for depression, fatigue, and long-term weight loss, but the FDA restricted amphetamine usage in 1970. Physicians may now only prescribe amphetamines for three medical conditions.

1. *Narcolepsy*: A condition that causes sudden sleeping; low doses of amphetamines enable narcoleptics to remain alert.
2. *Attention Deficit Hyperactivity Disorder (ADHD)*: A condition that may include attention difficulty, hyperactivity, and/or impulsiveness; Ritalin is a stimulant used for treatment.
3. *Obesity*: Short-term use of amphetamines in weight reduction programs; helps control appetite.

Medical use of amphetamines runs the risk of abuse potential and cardiovascular toxicities. Amphetamines increase heart rate, increase blood pressure, and damage veins and arteries, which may be especially fatal for patients with hypertension or heart arrhythmia.

Xanthines

Xanthines are alkaloids that can act to help open air passages in the lungs. As such they have been used in the treatment of asthma, bronchitis, emphysema, and other respiratory issues. They have also been used in treatment of apnea and chronic obstructive pulmonary disease. Some forms of xanthine, such as theophylline, can have toxic effects with use, and often have drug-drug and drug-condition interactions. There is a fine line between beneficial doses and doses that can produce toxic side effects.

Tolerance, Withdrawal, and Overdose

Withdrawal effects from cocaine depend on the amount of time a person has been a user and the intensity level of the abuse. Short-term withdrawal effects may include depression, insomnia, agitation, and drug cravings. **Anhedonia**, which is the inability to feel pleasure, is also a short-term effect of cocaine withdrawal. Long-term effects include mood swings and occasional cravings.

Overdose of amphetamines can cause restlessness, tremors, rapid breathing, panic, and aggression. It can promote nausea, vomiting, diarrhea, and fainting. Harmful side effects are most likely to occur when amphetamines are paired with alcohol. After continued use for a long period of time, coming down from amphetamines can be challenging. The body builds up a tolerance to the drug, and withdrawal symptoms will likely occur. Withdrawal can include aches and pains, confusion, irritability, restlessness, anxiety, depression, and paranoia.

Caffeine can produce tolerance and withdrawal symptoms as an individual could need increasing levels of a substance to produce the same effects of alertness. Continued use and subsequent cessation of use could result in symptoms of withdrawal. Caffeine withdrawal symptoms tend to be the opposite of the benefits of caffeine use—headaches, difficulty concentrating, irritability, and fatigue. Overdoses can occur in extremely high doses, such as 80 cups of coffee in one day; ingesting levels of caffeine this high could result in overdose and death.

Dependency Issues

Cocaine is a highly addictive drug that acts directly on the brain. Long-term use makes an individual more sensitive to the drug and its anxiety-producing effects. Users often go on binges, during which they use increasingly higher doses. Cocaine alters reactions in chronic users' brains so that even after a period of disuse, triggers can lead to relapse and overdose. Amphetamine use long-term can also cause dependency issues. Dependence can occur even if the prescription is taken according to doctor direction. Risk of amphetamine dependence increases if mental health issues exist, if there is a great deal of stress, if emotional problems are present, and if the individual has low self-esteem.

Prevention and Treatment

Acute toxicity treatment to prevent or treat overdose occurs in a medical setting. No clear-cut treatment program exists for cocaine or amphetamine addiction, but many people seek help from inpatient and outpatient facilities. Most treatments attempt to curb a person's craving for cocaine and to relieve mood swings. Counseling and support groups are typical elements of treating cocaine addiction. At this time there are no FDA-approved medications available to treat cocaine addiction, but recent brain imaging studies have shown which areas of the brain could be targeted in the development of treatment drugs. Individuals must distance themselves completely from others who use or supply any illicit drugs. Proximity to people who use can create triggers that cause instant strong cravings for the substance. It is also important to address issues with impulsivity, risk-taking, and rule-breaking, as these behaviors often lead to a return to use. Individuals must build a strong non-using support base of friends and family and occupy time with positive activities that do not involve drug use.

OPIOIDS

An **opioid**, also known as a **narcotic**, is any drug derived from opium, such as morphine and codeine, or any synthetic drug that has opium-like effects, such as oxycodone. Opioids act like two kinds of pain-suppressing neurotransmitters found naturally in the brain—enkephalins and endorphins. Although opioids are associated with drug abuse, they remain useful for therapeutic purposes because of their analgesic properties.

History and Types

Opium is a raw plant substance that contains both morphine and codeine, and its medical and recreational use dates back thousands of years to the Middle East. The introduction of opium poppies to China and India led to significant addiction problems. In 1729, China banned the sale of opium, but opium continued to be smuggled from India where it was primarily grown; the British government in India encouraged the profitable cultivation and smuggling of opium to China. Trade disputes and conflicts between the Chinese and British governments triggered the Opium War, which lasted from 1839 until 1842. In 1803, Frederick Serturner extracted and isolated the main active ingredient in opium, which was ten times more potent than the opium itself. Serturner named his extraction morphine. Thirty years later, codeine was extracted from the poppy plant. In 1874, Bayer Laboratories made changes to the morphine molecule to create heroin, which has three times the potency of morphine. Initially, the medical community was unaware of dependency issues associated with heroin, but federal laws were enacted in the early 1900s to regulate heroin.

Effects

Opioids provide relief from pain and provide a sense of euphoria that make them highly addictive. Opioids affect the brain regions involved in reward and act on cell receptors to reduce the perception of pain. Many opioids are prescribed as a pain medication after a medical procedure or for injury. Unfortunately, the highly addictive nature of the opioids makes even legal use monitored by a doctor very risky, as individuals seek to extend or intensify the feelings of euphoria. For individuals with chronic pain, this can become even more tempting. Constipation is one of the most common side effects of opioids, but other side effects include drowsiness, respiratory depression, nausea, and itching. Opioids have been used to treat severe diarrhea, especially in patients with dysentery.

Uses and Administration

Opioids have historically been used as painkillers, dispensed legally through prescription. The following table summarizes different types of opioids and their medicinal uses:

Methods of Using Opioids	
Opioid	Medical Use
Morphine	Used to relieve moderate to severe pain without inducing sleep
Codeine	Used for treating mild to moderate pain and as a cough suppressant
Fentanyls	Synthetic opioids that are highly potent; used for general anesthesia and chronic pain
Oxycodone	Analgesic used for severe pain related to cancer or other lingering diseases

Opioid	Medical Use
Dextromethorphan	Synthetic used in OTC cough medicines; high doses may cause hallucinations
Buprenorphine	Analgesic used to treat narcotic abuse and dependence; low potential for dependence
Meperidine	Synthetic drug used to treat moderate pain; associated with dependence

For some, the use of opioids comes with a heavy price. Drug enforcement agents report that many who turn to heroin begin with hydrocodone. Hydrocodone is often prescribed by a doctor in pill form, yet these pills have a high street value and often end up for sale. Unfortunately, hydrocodone, oxycodone, morphine, and codeine are expensive on the street, leading the way to heroin. Heroin comes in powder form and is crushed and mixed with other substances. It is diluted with water, heated to liquid form, and injected intravenously. Fentanyl, which has recently been mixed with heroin with fatal results, is another form of opioid. Fentanyl is often prescribed as a transdermal method of pain relief. In its intended form it provides a slow release of medication, but delayed onset of action and side effects can lead to problems that are not quickly reversed. Opioids can also be administered sublingually or subcutaneously for slow and controlled relief.

Tolerance, Withdrawal, and Overdose

Unlike morphine and codeine, which may be used for medical purposes, heroin cannot be prescribed or used in any US clinics. Heroin is deadly and the most likely opioid to be abused. All opioids have the potential for abuse because they cause tolerance, dependence, and withdrawal effects. Opioids prescribed for pain relief will require increased doses to maintain the needed effect, and recreational users will need additional amounts to achieve the desired euphoria. Physical dependence on opioids is likely for people who use high doses on a regular basis.

The initial stage of heroin usage brings euphoria and positive effects that encourage further abuse. Later stages require users to continue taking the drug to avoid withdrawal symptoms. Most heroin users inject themselves three or four times each day because withdrawal signs usually begin 6 hours after each dose.

The following is a list of withdrawal symptoms associated with opioid abuse:

- **6 hours after last dose:** anxiety and drug cravings
- **14 hours after last dose:** runny nose, perspiration, and yawning
- **16 hours after last dose:** pupil dilation, tremors, hot and cold flashes, and achiness
- **24–36 hours after last dose:** insomnia, nausea, and increased blood pressure, temperature, and pulse
- **36–48 hours after last dose:** vomiting, diarrhea, and increased blood sugar

Each withdrawal symptom builds on the previous one, so, by the final stage, a person may experience all of the effects at once. Opioid withdrawal is not typically life-threatening, but it is extremely painful. Withdrawal from methadone, which is a long-lasting synthetic opioid, is associated with the first three symptoms but with less severity. Craving for methadone does not begin until 24 hours after the last dose, which is why oral methadone is often employed in the treatment of heroin dependency. Although methadone causes dependence as well, it is less addictive than heroin and easier to manage. However, buprenorphine has a lower risk of dependence than methadone and provides an alternative form of treatment for heroin addicts.

Dependency Issues

The presence of severe withdrawal symptoms often reduces an individual's willingness to stop use. The individual will also experience severe cravings for the substance. These factors make it very hard for an individual to psychologically separate from the substance, and physical issues such as diarrhea and vomiting, cold flashes, and muscle pain decrease motivation to quit. Individuals addicted to opioids are often willing to lie, cheat, and steal in order to maintain the physical and psychological dependence on the substance. They are willing to lose family and home in order to continue use. This makes treatment very challenging.

Prevention and Treatment

Some studies indicate the use of the prescription opioids Vicodin and Oxy-Contin could be the gateway to heroin use. Prevention programs target younger populations in an effort to stop the use before it starts. Since opioid addiction can be so pervasive, it is often treated with the use of other drugs designed to mimic the effects and reduce the lethality while incorporating mental health treatment options. Inpatient treatment is often recommended in order to monitor health with medications and surround the individual with supportive, knowledgeable help and therapy. Individuals often explore attitudes and behaviors related to drug use and learn new and healthier means of living and problem solving.

CANNABINOIDS

Marijuana has properties similar to a variety of substances, so it is typically given its own classification. Marijuana has been described as a depressant, hallucinogenic, and an analgesic, which makes it a unique substance. The chief psychoactive ingredient of marijuana, **delta-9-tetrahydrocannabinol (THC)**, is found in the resin of the *Cannabis sativa* plant, especially in the flowering tops of female plants. The woody fibers of the cannabis stem are used to make hemp cloth and rope.

History and Types

Cannabis plants have been cultivated for thousands of years since the discovery that smoking the dried and crushed leaves produced intoxicating effects. Marijuana has a history of usage in India as part of religious ceremonies. The use of marijuana spread from India to the rest of the world: Asia, Africa, Europe, and the Americas. During the 1930s in the United States, public concerns were raised about marijuana as a cause of violent crimes. Although little evidence supported a link between marijuana and violence, the substance was outlawed in 1937. During the 1960s and 1970s, marijuana served as a symbol for rejecting authority, and its usage peaked in 1980.

Effects

Marijuana contains over 400 chemicals, but THC is the most active one. When marijuana is smoked, THC is absorbed rapidly into the blood, distributed into the brain, and then redistributed to the rest of the body. Within 5 to 10 minutes, a user experiences the peak psychological and cardiovascular effects of the drug, and within 30 minutes most of the THC is out of the brain. However, reduced percentages of THC linger in a user's body for days, and large doses may take weeks to eliminate from the body. THC taken orally absorbs slowly and incompletely, so it takes longer for a user to experience its effects. The THC level in marijuana varies, but most marijuana sold by dealers in the United States has a THC content of 0.5–11 percent. Such levels are believed to be 20 percent greater than marijuana that was smoked in the 1960s and 1970s because of more efficient cultivation methods. **Hashish**, which is another derivative of cannabis, contains the purest version of the plant's resin. Hashish has THC levels anywhere from 3.6–25 percent, so it is a more potent version of marijuana that may generate hallucinogenic effects.

Marijuana affects both the body and the mind in a variety of ways. The primary and most consistent physiological effect of marijuana usage is an increased heart rate. Other bodily effects include reddening of the eyes and drying of the mouth and throat. Low doses of marijuana typically produce feelings of euphoria, tranquility, and relaxation. Loss of coordination and balance and slowed reaction times often accompany marijuana usage as well, which is why driving or operating heavy machinery is extremely dangerous after using marijuana. Marijuana users also experience an increased appetite.

The "high" experienced from smoking one marijuana cigarette usually lasts 2 or 3 hours and may be accompanied by impaired memory and an altered perception of time and events. In contrast, smoking a larger dose of marijuana may result in anxiety, panic, hallucinations, delusions, and paranoia, especially with people who are already feeling anxious or depressed.

Long-term effects of heavy marijuana usage are inconclusive. However, experts agree that long-term smoking of marijuana decreases pulmonary capabilities, causes chronic lung diseases, and raises the risk of lung cancer. Whether or not there are long-term cognitive effects of marijuana usage is a controversial subject. Some studies have shown that heavy marijuana usage causes **amotivational syndrome**, a psychological condition marked by decreased motivation and productivity, problems with concentration and memory, and disinterest in normal social activities. Critics of these studies, however, argue that there is no direct correlation between marijuana usage and amotivational syndrome, and some even argue that the syndrome is nonexistent. Frequent high doses of marijuana produce tolerance, so higher doses are needed to achieve effects of similar intensity. In addition, mild physical dependence can develop in people who often use high doses of marijuana, but physical dependence is typically very low. Mild withdrawal symptoms may include irritability, insomnia, and loss of appetite.

Uses and Administration

Questions continue to arise regarding the medical use of marijuana. Advocates of using marijuana for medical purposes assert that the substance has many possible applications. The FDA approved Marinol, a legal form of synthetic THC that is available in a capsule by prescription, to treat nausea associated with cancer chemotherapy and to stimulate the appetite of HIV/AIDS patients. However, marijuana legalization supporters claim that THC is more effective when it is smoked and that medical conditions like migraines, depression, and seizures could be relieved by smoking marijuana. However, critics point out that smoking is a poor delivery system for medication because of questionable dosage regulation and possible pulmonary damage. Limited studies are available regarding the actual medical benefits or potential dangers of marijuana, so the controversy is likely to continue.

Tolerance, Withdrawal, and Overdose

Marijuana is rarely addictive, and while instances of withdrawal have been reported, many health officials do not acknowledge this. Synthetic cannabinoids, on the other hand, are addictive and can cause withdrawal symptoms of headaches, anxiety, depression, and irritability. They can raise blood pressure and affect the blood supply to the heart, in some cases resulting in death.

Dependency Issues

At this time, cannabis is not recognized as a drug that produces life-threatening risks and does not meet the criteria for dependency. While it can have a negative impact on an individual's physiological and psychological health when it is taken regularly in larger quantities, many of the more lethal risks are secondary, such as driving under the influence and getting into an accident.

Prevention and Treatment

Treatment of cannabinoid abuse tends to follow the same path as treatment of other drugs, including counseling. Medications have not been tested for treatment of cannabinoid abuse to a great extent and, as such, are not approved for treatment.

Current Trends

Regulation as well as public and medical views of marijuana have undergone significant changes in recent years as both medical bodies and state legislatures have begun to re-evaluate the drug's uses and opportunities. In recent years, the American Medical Association (AMA) has called for marijuana to be reclassified on the DEA Drug Schedule, removing it from Schedule I so that it is more readily available for research purposes. Early research has proved promising for medical benefits. Simultaneously, states have assessed the regulatory cost of the drug's criminalization, and as a result, marijuana has seen significant deregulation. In 2010, only 25 states allowed medical usage of marijuana. Currently, states that maintain complete illegal status are in the minority. Most states allow some form of medical usage, and multiple states have fully legalized the drug, allowing citizens to access it for both medical and recreational purposes, effectively decriminalizing possession, use, cultivation, transportation, and distribution. These states include California, Colorado, Illinois, Maine, Massachusetts, Michigan, Nevada, Oregon, Washington, and Vermont.

Decriminalization has allowed states to capitalize on the growing industry and intake significant tax revenue to fund local initiatives, including transportation projects and education funding. While federal law still maintains marijuana as an illicit substance, the legal landscape has shifted significantly across most state governments. In the early 2010s, several federal policies expressly allowed state-based marijuana operations to continue as long as state regulations were strictly adhered to. Such policies have been terminated in recent years, but such reversals have yet to lead to prosecution. The clash between federal and state law has created precarious positions for the cannabis industry. Certain elements of business are complicated by the gray legal status with benefits from banking and tax code limited by federal statutes. However, with strong economic opportunities and shifting public and medical opinions, it's likely that the industry will keep growing, and the trend toward legalization will continue barring crackdowns at the federal level.

HALLUCINOGENS

History and Types

For many centuries, medicine men, shamans, and mystics have used hallucinogenic plants and herbs as part of spiritual events in different cultures around the world. Hallucinogens, such as LSD, are substances that generate perceptual disturbances and produce visions for those who use them. Since many substances generate hallucinogenic effects at certain doses, the determination of whether a drug is classified as a hallucinogen has been debated for many years. In general, a drug's tendency to produce hallucinations places it in the hallucinogen category.

Within the hallucinogen classification, there are variations. **Phantastica hallucinogens** are those that create a fantasy world for the user, and they are divided into two categories: **indole** and **catechol**. Phantastica hallucinogens are also known as **psychedelic** and **psychotomimetic drugs**.

Phantastica Hallucinogens	
Type	**Description**
Indole hallucinogens	Indole is a chemical structure found in the neurotransmitter serotonin and also in LSD and psilocybin, which is derived from the Mexican mushroom.
Catechol hallucinogens	Catecholamines include the neurotransmitters norepinephrine, epinephrine, and dopamine, and they are found in the peyote cactus, which contains mescaline.

In 1938, Dr. Albert Hofmann, a Swiss scientist, discovered **lysergic acid diethylamide (LSD)** while searching for active chemicals in ergot compounds. Ergot is a type of fungus that grows in rye and other plants. Hofmann's synthetic drug became one of the most widely known hallucinogenic drugs.

Effects

The effects associated with using LSD are typical of many other hallucinogenic substances, including peyote, but effects vary, depending upon the individual and the environment. The following is a list of possible effects related to LSD usage:

- Hallucinations
- Heightened sensory awareness
- Enhanced emotions
- Exaggeration of perceptions
- Awareness of both fantasy world and real world
- Time distortion
- Awareness of inner thought

Hallucinogens such as LSD and peyote have similar effects and do not cause psychological or physical dependence. **Phencyclidine (PCP)**, also known as **angel dust**, is a different kind of hallucinogen that does cause psychological dependence. Originally developed in the 1950s as an anesthetic, PCP generates a number of unique effects:

- Numbness in low doses and unconsciousness in higher doses
- Coma, fever, seizures, and death linked to high doses
- Altered body perception and feelings of strength, power, and invincibility
- Schizophrenic-type episodes that may include violent behavior

Uses and Administration

Hallucinogens are ingested in a variety of forms, including tablets or pills, liquid, raw or dried plant, tea, snorting, injecting, inhaling, and absorption in the mouth. In some cases, the plant is ground into a powder, and in others it is soaked into a piece of paper that is then placed in the mouth. The rate of absorption depends on the method of ingestion and often begins between 20 and 90 minutes after administration. The effects can last up to 12 hours.

Tolerance, Withdrawal, and Overdose

Addiction to hallucinogens is not universal and is still the subject of research. Because there tend to be significant differences between classic hallucinogens (LSD, psilocybin, DMT) and dissociative drugs (PCP), even tolerance, withdrawal, and overdosing vary. Use of certain substances, such as LSD, can lead to tolerance that requires higher doses to achieve the desired effects. Regular use of certain classic hallucinogens can also lead to tolerance for other substances. Withdrawal is dependent on the substance taken; PCP users report drug cravings, headaches, and sweating after stopping usage. Further, overdose is less common with hallucinogens, with high doses resulting in unpleasant experiences; however, high doses of dissociative drugs, such as PCP, can lead to seizures, coma, and death. When combined with depressants, PCP use is more likely to lead to coma. The most significant danger of repeated and high-dose use of hallucinogens comes with the altered states of perception and mood that can result in dangerous user behavior—elevation of suicidal feelings or misperception of environmental dangers.

OTHER DRUGS OF ABUSE

Anabolic Steroids

Androgens are a group of hormones frequently abused by athletes. **Testosterone** is the primary natural androgen responsible for growth spurts during adolescence, as well as the growth of the male sex organs, body hair, muscles, and vocal cords. **Anabolic steroids** are a type of steroid hormone related to the male hormone testosterone. Male and female athletes have abused anabolic steroids in the attempt to build muscle mass and improve physical performance. The negative side effects of taking high doses of anabolic steroids include muscle tears, increased aggression, uncontrolled rage, headaches, insomnia, and anxiety. The use of anabolic steroids is banned by nearly all major sporting organizations.

Over-the-Counter (OTC) Substances

Over-the-counter substances can be addictive and dangerous when used improperly. Cold and cough medicines taken in large doses can create a high and cause hallucinations. This can also cause vomiting, rapid heart rate, and sometimes brain damage in extreme cases. Decongestants are also abused; pseudoephedrine, for example, contains the active ingredient used to make methamphetamine.

Synthetic Substances

Synthetic drugs are substances that are constructed of man-made chemicals that are added to plant material in some way, often through spray. They are then marketed as legal highs that mimic marijuana. Synthetic drugs can be called "synthetic marijuana," "K2," or "Spice." They are often marketed legally as herbal incense, potpourri, bath salts, or jewelry cleaner. **Synthetic cannabinoids** are the second most frequently used illegal drug reported by high school students; they are second to marijuana.

Synthetic cathinones are man-made chemicals that mimic amphetamines. The contents of both synthetic cannabinoids and cathinones are constantly changing as the manufacturing process has no restrictions or regulations. This leads to risk of accidental poisoning, severe anxiety, nausea, vomiting, racing heart, hallucinations, and increased suicide risk. Synthetic cathinone causes adverse side effects similar to the amphetamines it mimics, and it can cause the same paranoia, delusions, and violent behavior.

Synthetic substances are labeled "not for human consumption" in an effort to avoid regulation by the FDA. The synthetic substances are available in retail stores and online, and federal agencies are working to ban many of them. The Synthetic Drug Abuse Prevention Act of 2012 placed twenty-six types of synthetic mixtures into the Schedule I tier of controlled substances, which allows drug enforcement agents to take harsh action to remove supply.

Club Drugs

Club drugs are those associated with all-night raves, parties, bars, and nightclubs. The club drug group includes MDMA (Ecstasy), GHB, and Rohypnol. **MDMA** is a synthetic amphetamine that gained popularity among young adults at raves and nightclubs in England and the United States. The effects of MDMA include increased empathy, distortions of time, increased energy, and euphoria. A number of psychiatrists advocate the use of MDMA for the treatment of mental disorders such as fear and anxiety. Inconclusive laboratory studies of MDMA have shown that the drug may cause brain damage.

Gamma hydroxybutyrate (GHB) is found naturally in the body and has a structure similar to the inhibitory neurotransmitter GABA. GHB is a depressant that has been used as an anesthetic and a dietary supplement. Athletes have used GHB as a way to stimulate muscle growth. GHB is considered a club drug because it has been linked to date rape. Clear and odorless, GHB can be easily mixed with the beverage of an unsuspecting victim. The substance has amnesiac and sedative characteristics that make victims vulnerable to sexual predators. Legal prosecution is often hindered because victims cannot recall details of the crime and the substance leaves the bloodstream quickly.

Rohypnol, which is illegal in the United States, is a benzodiazepine. Benzodiazepines are depressants taken for anxiety and sleep. Rohypnol is linked to date rapes. Sexual predators dissolve the drug in a victim's drink, and sexual assault victims are unable to recall any specific details because Rohypnol blocks short-term memory.

ANTIPSYCHOTIC DRUGS

History and Types

A group of drugs called **phenothiazines** was introduced in the 1950s as a way to treat psychosis. These **antipsychotics**, or **neuroleptics**, revolutionized the mental healthcare system by reducing the need for physical restraints and electroshock treatment of unmanageable patients. Antipsychotics decrease psychotic symptoms without sedation and enable patients to remain subdued enough to take care of their physical needs and to participate in social activities. Phenothiazines have been shown to help most schizophrenics, although the drugs are not a cure. Discontinuing the medication leads to a relapse of most symptoms, but the situation can be reversed by resuming treatment. **Typical (first-generation) antipsychotic drugs** include haloperidol and chlorpromazine. Some types of **atypical (second-generation) antipsychotic drugs** include risperidone, quetiapine, olanzapine, clozapine, and aripiprazole.

Effects

Antipsychotic drugs act to take away many of the symptoms of such psychotic illnesses as schizophrenia. They do not cure psychotic illnesses, but they do make the symptoms milder, and sometimes they can shorten the course of a current psychotic episode. Newer atypical antipsychotics have fewer side effects than the older antipsychotics and are often used first. Some of these drugs take effect quickly, easing symptoms within the first day. Antipsychotics are not addictive, but they have some side effects. Movement disorders similar to Parkinson's disease, such as hand tremors, muscular rigidity, and a shuffling stride, may occur with patients taking antipsychotics. Most side effects of antipsychotics are mild, but there are some risks. One atypical antipsychotic, clozapine, can cause a serious blood disorder, which means patients on this drug must have their blood tested every week or so. Weight gain is also a side effect of the medications, which could require adjustments to diet and exercise. One significant risk is that when patients begin to feel better, some decide to stop taking the medication. This signals a return of the symptoms that were controlled by the medication. Maintenance treatment is often required, although it is important to determine what other medications an individual might be on. Some drug interactions can occur, leading to increased depression or interference with the medicinal value of the other medications. Long-term use can result in tardive dyskinesia, a condition characterized by tics or involuntary motions.

Uses and Administration

Antipsychotics are obtained with a prescription for certain mental health issues. Unfortunately, some individuals have discovered that they can be used to enhance the effects of illicit substances. For this purpose, individuals might obtain the drugs through improper prescription practices or through someone who sells them illegally.

ANTIDEPRESSANTS AND MOOD STABILIZERS

Depression is one of the most common psychiatric disorders and is characterized by sleep disturbances, diminished pleasure in normal activities, feelings of guilt and pessimism, and, in severe cases, suicidal thoughts. **Antidepressant medication** is typically prescribed to patients who have endogenous major depression, which is caused by either a genetic disorder or imbalanced brain chemistry.

History and Types

Antidepressant drugs were discovered in the 1950s as researchers sought a treatment for schizophrenia. They created a drug that was able to control mood, pain, and other sensations. This did not help patients with schizophrenia, but it did help patients with depression. This first form of antidepressant was categorized as **tricyclics**. Tricyclics helped many who experienced symptoms of depression, but side effects prompted exploration for a different form. The second type of antidepressants were **monoamine oxidase inhibitors (MAOIs)**, which were effective but again carried some serious side effects. In the late 1980s, drug research was able to produce a new form of antidepressants termed **selective reuptake inhibitors (SSRIs)**. The SSRIs did not produce the serious side effects of the first two forms. The SSRIs more specifically targeted the neurotransmitter serotonin and proved to be just as effective as tricyclics and monoamine oxidase inhibitors.[4]

----

4. Fitzpatrick, L. (2010). A brief history of antidepressants. Retrieved from: http://content.time.com/time/health/article/0,8599,1952143,00.html

Types of Antidepressants

Antidepressant	Effects and Examples
Monoamine oxidase inhibitors (MAOIs)	Limited use because of significant side effects when combined with food, wine, and other medications. Side effects include dizziness, headaches, and trembling. Drugs in this group include phenelzine (Nardil) and tranylcypromine (Parnate).
Selective reuptake inhibitors (SSRIs)	Considered safer than other types; fewest side effects. Prozac is the most prescribed; other brands include Paxil, Zoloft, and Celexa.
Tricyclics	Side effects include drowsiness, dry mouth, and blurred vision; patients develop tolerance. Drugs in this group include amitriptyline (Elavil), imipramine (Tofranil), doxepin (Sinequan), and nortriptyline (Pamelor).

Effects

Antidepressants work by making either norepinephrine or serotonin more readily available to the brain. Despite the differences between the three types of antidepressants, patients who take any of them typically do not see improvements in mood for approximately two weeks. The medication reaches a patient's brain quickly, but experts believe that repeated exposure to antidepressant medication is necessary before symptoms of depression diminish. Antidepressants can cause some unpleasant side effects, including nervousness, headache, and upset stomach. These side effects often fade over the course of time as the individual's body system gets used to the drug. There have also been links between antidepressants and suicide and violent behaviors.

Uses and Administration

Antidepressants normally come in pill form and are prescribed by a physician. SSRIs are considered nonaddictive, but they can create a dependency with continual overuse, especially when the user crushes and inhales the drug. Antidepressants act to restore balance in neurotransmitters involved in regulating mood, including serotonin, norepinephrine, and dopamine.

Choice of antidepressant often relies on potential side effects based on an individual's physical status. Antidepressants are used with a wide range of ages, including children as young as 12 years old. Some believe that antidepressants are overprescribed and mental health therapy is underused. There is a need to approach treatment of depression from both physical and psychological forms in order to minimize risk of suicide and increase efficacy of treatment.

Tolerance and Withdrawal

Dependency can arise with consistent abuse of antidepressants, and an individual will likely experience side effects if he or she ends use quickly. Side effects can include tremors, insomnia, nausea, fatigue, drowsiness, and dizziness. Some studies have indicated symptoms of tolerance and withdrawal with discontinued use of antidepressants after long-term use. Recurrent bouts of depression have been indicated as a long-term situation that increases risk of relapse, reduces antidepressant efficacy, and increases tolerance and withdrawal risk. Addiction to antidepressants can also have psychological side effects, including suicidal thoughts, increased depression, psychosis, and confusion. Some evidence suggests that SSRIs can, in some cases, increase suicidality, with a higher risk in children and adolescents who use them. The cause of this increased risk is still under investigation, although theories propose that it might be the result of the increased energy to act that occurs with SSRI use occurring before individuals are psychologically stable. Thus, they feel physically able to perform activities, but psychologically they are still in a great deal of pain they want to end.

SUMMING IT UP

- **Drugs** are natural or artificial substances that improve, obstruct, or alter mind and body functions. **Illicit drugs**, such as marijuana and cocaine, are illegal to possess. **Licit (legal) drugs** include caffeine, alcohol, nicotine, and over-the-counter (OTC) drugs like cold remedies. Alcohol and nicotine are considered **gateway drugs** because most illicit drug abusers first try liquor and/or cigarettes.
- **Psychoactive drugs** mainly affect the central nervous system, and they result in changes to consciousness, thought processes, and mood.

- **Drug dependency** occurs when one uses a drug so often that going without it is physically and psychologically difficult and results in such withdrawal symptoms as nausea, anxiety, muscle spasms, and sweating.
    - ⊚ The three models of dependency are **moral, disease,** and **characterological** or **personality predisposition.**
    - ⊚ Theories of dependency are **biological, psychological,** and **sociological.**
- Drug classifications are **stimulants** (cocaine, amphetamines, Ritalin, caffeine), **depressants** (alcohol, barbiturates, sleeping pills, inhalants), **hallucinogens** (LSD, mescaline, Ecstasy, PCP), **opioids** (opium, morphine, codeine, heroin, methadone), **cannabis** (marijuana, THC, hashish), **nicotine** (cigarettes, chewing tobacco, cigars), and **psychotherapeutics** (Prozac, Haldol).
- When drugs are ingested in the body, they interact with the **cell receptors** of certain cells and change the function of those cells. This interaction results in changes in body function and behavior.
- The human body constantly attempts to maintain internal stability, a process known as **homeostasis.** Homeostatic mechanisms regulate body temperature, blood pressure, and glucose concentrations, as well as many other physiological functions.
- The **nervous system** is composed of **neurons,** which are specialized nerve cells that transfer messages throughout the body.
    - ⊚ The brain's billions of neurons communicate with each other by releasing chemical messengers known as **neurotransmitters.**
    - ⊚ The nervous system is divided into the **somatic, autonomic,** and **central nervous systems.**
- The three main types of **drug interactions** are **additive, antagonistic,** and **synergistic.**
    - ⊚ A **potentiating effect** is a type of synergistic interaction.
    - ⊚ Any combination of depressants, alcohol, or narcotics can lead to respiratory failure and death.
- **Blood alcohol content (BAC)** estimates are based on a person's gender, weight, and alcohol consumption. A BAC level greater than 0.08 percent is illegal in every US state. A BAC level of 0.4–0.6 percent is often lethal, as breathing can stop.
- Withdrawal effects from alcohol and barbiturates are more severe than withdrawal from other substances. The **four states of withdrawal** start with **tremors, insomnia,** and **rapid heartbeat** and end with life-threatening **seizures.**
- **Sedative-hypnotics,** also known as **central nervous system (CNS) depressants,** reduce CNS activity, decrease the brain's level of awareness, and relieve anxiety.

- The **three categories of inhalants** are **gaseous anesthetics**, **nitrites**, and **volatile solvents**.
  - ◉ Inhaling methods include sniffing or snorting, bagging, and huffing.
- **Nicotine** is a colorless, volatile liquid alkaloid that is highly addictive. Nicotine decreases ability of blood to carry oxygen; increases blood pressure, heart rate, and blood flow; and diminishes one's desire to eat for a short time.
  - ◉ **Passive smoke** is the cigarette smoke in the environment inhaled by nonsmokers.
  - ◉ **Mainstream smoke** is drawn in directly from the mouthpiece of a cigarette.
  - ◉ **Sidestream** or **secondhand smoke** comes from the lighted end of a cigarette.
- **Stimulants** (uppers) increase energy levels and generate a euphoric state for users. Cocaine and amphetamines are stimulants. Cocaine use includes chewing coca leaves, snorting, intravenous, and smoking crack cocaine. Amphetamines can increase heart rate and blood pressure and damage veins and arteries.
- **Opioids** or **narcotics** are drugs derived from opium that suppress pain and include morphine, codeine, Fentanyl, oxycodone, dextromethorphan, buprenorphine, and meperidine.
- **Heroin** is the most likely opioid to be abused and can be deadly.
- **Marijuana**, a depressant, hallucinogenic, and analgesic, is a unique substance. Its chief psychoactive ingredient, **delta-9-tetrahydrocannabinol (THC)**, is found in the resin of the cannabis sativa plant.
  - ◉ **Hashish**, another derivative of cannabis, has THC levels of 3.6–25 percent, making it a more potent version of marijuana that may generate hallucinogenic effects.
- **Hallucinogens**, such as LSD, are substances that generate perceptual disturbances and produce visions for those who use them.
- **Phantastica hallucinogens** create a fantasy world for the user and are divided into two categories: **indole** and **catechol**.
- **Synthetic drugs** are substances that are constructed of man-made chemicals that are added to plant material in some way, often through a spray.
- **Club drugs** are those associated with all-night raves, parties, bars, and nightclubs. The club drug group includes MDMA (Ecstasy), GHB, and Rohypnol.
- **Anabolic steroids** are related to the male hormone testosterone and have been abused by athletes wanting to build muscle mass and improve physical performance. Negative side effects include muscle tears, uncontrolled rage, insomnia, and anxiety.

- **Phenothiazines**, or **antipsychotic drugs**, decrease psychotic symptoms without sedation, allowing patients to participate in social activities. Phenothiazines help most schizophrenics but are not a cure.
- **Antidepressants** can be divided into three main categories: **tricyclics, monoamine oxidase inhibitors (MAOIs)**, and **selective reuptake inhibitors (SSRIs)**.

Chapter 4

Substance Abuse Post-Test

POST-TEST ANSWER SHEET

1. Ⓐ Ⓑ Ⓒ Ⓓ   17. Ⓐ Ⓑ Ⓒ Ⓓ   33. Ⓐ Ⓑ Ⓒ Ⓓ

2. Ⓐ Ⓑ Ⓒ Ⓓ   18. Ⓐ Ⓑ Ⓒ Ⓓ   34. Ⓐ Ⓑ Ⓒ Ⓓ

3. Ⓐ Ⓑ Ⓒ Ⓓ   19. Ⓐ Ⓑ Ⓒ Ⓓ   35. Ⓐ Ⓑ Ⓒ Ⓓ

4. Ⓐ Ⓑ Ⓒ Ⓓ   20. Ⓐ Ⓑ Ⓒ Ⓓ   36. Ⓐ Ⓑ Ⓒ Ⓓ

5. Ⓐ Ⓑ Ⓒ Ⓓ   21. Ⓐ Ⓑ Ⓒ Ⓓ   37. Ⓐ Ⓑ Ⓒ Ⓓ

6. Ⓐ Ⓑ Ⓒ Ⓓ   22. Ⓐ Ⓑ Ⓒ Ⓓ   38. Ⓐ Ⓑ Ⓒ Ⓓ

7. Ⓐ Ⓑ Ⓒ Ⓓ   23. Ⓐ Ⓑ Ⓒ Ⓓ   39. Ⓐ Ⓑ Ⓒ Ⓓ

8. Ⓐ Ⓑ Ⓒ Ⓓ   24. Ⓐ Ⓑ Ⓒ Ⓓ   40. Ⓐ Ⓑ Ⓒ Ⓓ

9. Ⓐ Ⓑ Ⓒ Ⓓ   25. Ⓐ Ⓑ Ⓒ Ⓓ   41. Ⓐ Ⓑ Ⓒ Ⓓ

10. Ⓐ Ⓑ Ⓒ Ⓓ   26. Ⓐ Ⓑ Ⓒ Ⓓ   42. Ⓐ Ⓑ Ⓒ Ⓓ

11. Ⓐ Ⓑ Ⓒ Ⓓ   27. Ⓐ Ⓑ Ⓒ Ⓓ   43. Ⓐ Ⓑ Ⓒ Ⓓ

12. Ⓐ Ⓑ Ⓒ Ⓓ   28. Ⓐ Ⓑ Ⓒ Ⓓ   44. Ⓐ Ⓑ Ⓒ Ⓓ

13. Ⓐ Ⓑ Ⓒ Ⓓ   29. Ⓐ Ⓑ Ⓒ Ⓓ   45. Ⓐ Ⓑ Ⓒ Ⓓ

14. Ⓐ Ⓑ Ⓒ Ⓓ   30. Ⓐ Ⓑ Ⓒ Ⓓ   46. Ⓐ Ⓑ Ⓒ Ⓓ

15. Ⓐ Ⓑ Ⓒ Ⓓ   31. Ⓐ Ⓑ Ⓒ Ⓓ   47. Ⓐ Ⓑ Ⓒ Ⓓ

16. Ⓐ Ⓑ Ⓒ Ⓓ   32. Ⓐ Ⓑ Ⓒ Ⓓ   48. Ⓐ Ⓑ Ⓒ Ⓓ

49. Ⓐ Ⓑ Ⓒ Ⓓ   **53.** Ⓐ Ⓑ Ⓒ Ⓓ   **57.** Ⓐ Ⓑ Ⓒ Ⓓ

50. Ⓐ Ⓑ Ⓒ Ⓓ   **54.** Ⓐ Ⓑ Ⓒ Ⓓ   **58.** Ⓐ Ⓑ Ⓒ Ⓓ

51. Ⓐ Ⓑ Ⓒ Ⓓ   **55.** Ⓐ Ⓑ Ⓒ Ⓓ   **59.** Ⓐ Ⓑ Ⓒ Ⓓ

52. Ⓐ Ⓑ Ⓒ Ⓓ   **56.** Ⓐ Ⓑ Ⓒ Ⓓ   **60.** Ⓐ Ⓑ Ⓒ Ⓓ

SUBSTANCE ABUSE POST-TEST
72 minutes—60 questions

Directions: Carefully read each of the following 60 questions. Choose the best answer to each question and fill in the corresponding circle on the answer sheet. The Answer Key and Explanations can be found following this post-test.

---

1. Amphetamines may be prescribed for which of the following medical conditions?

    A. Depression
    B. Asthma
    C. Epilepsy
    D. ADHD

2. The process used to make whiskey that involves heating an alcoholic mixture and collecting the vapors is known as

    A. fermentation.
    B. inhalation.
    C. distillation.
    D. prohibition.

3. How long do the effects of hallucinogens tend to last?

    A. Up to 12 hours
    B. Up to 16 hours
    C. Up to 20 hours
    D. Up to 24 hours

4. How long does a treatment plan normally last?

    A. 30 days
    B. 45 days
    C. 60 days
    D. 90 days

5. A side effect of antipsychotic drugs is

   A. short-term memory loss.
   B. suicidal thoughts.
   C. hand tremors.
   D. depression.

6. Of the following, the substance with the lowest possibility of physical dependency is

   A. methadone.
   B. marijuana.
   C. alcohol.
   D. codeine.

7. The most commonly used illicit drug in the United States is

   A. barbiturates.
   B. marijuana.
   C. cocaine.
   D. alcohol.

8. Which of the following statements is accurate?

   A. Bromides replaced barbiturates as a safer anti-anxiety alternative.
   B. Benzodiazepines are safe and do not produce any withdrawal or dependency effects.
   C. Most illicit use of anti-anxiety drugs is the result of private manufacture and sale.
   D. Prescriptions drugs can be just as dangerous as illicit drugs.

9. According to the moral model of drug dependency, people are dependent on drugs because of

   A. peer pressure.
   B. personal choices.
   C. personality traits.
   D. biological conditions.

10. The original concept behind the temperance movement was

   A. alcohol abstinence.
   B. marijuana legalization.
   C. drinking in moderation.
   D. prohibition of smoking.

11. Which part of the neuron is responsible for carrying a message across the synapse from one neuron to the next?

   A. Cell body
   B. Neurotransmitter
   C. Dendrite
   D. Axon

12. Which schedule of drugs can be dispensed without a prescription?

   A. Schedule II
   B. Schedule III
   C. Schedule IV
   D. Schedule V

13. Which of the following neurotransmitters would include an indole chemical structure?

   A. Norepinephrine
   B. Dopamine
   C. Epinephrine
   D. Serotonin

14. Which of the following was the first known abused inhalant?

   A. Amyl nitrite
   B. Ether
   C. Nitrous oxide
   D. Chloroform

15. Withdrawal symptoms are most associated with

   A. drug misuse.
   B. substance abuse.
   C. psychoactive drugs.
   D. drug dependency.

16. The primary active ingredient in marijuana is

   A. THC.
   B. MDMA.
   C. cannabis.
   D. Marinol.

17. All of the following factors increase a smoker's risk of having cancer EXCEPT:

    A. Daily number of cigarettes smoked
    B. Number of years spent smoking
    C. Gender and body weight
    D. Age when smoking began

18. Prohibition laws led to

    A. decreased criminal activity.
    B. dependence upon narcotics.
    C. reduction in alcohol usage.
    D. black market alcohol sales.

19. Which of the following is an effect associated with cocaine withdrawal?

    A. Heavy sweating
    B. Deadening of taste buds
    C. Life-threatening seizures
    D. Inability to feel pleasure

20. Which of the following is true of cannabinoids?

    A. The high from smoking a marijuana cigarette lasts about 6 to 7 hours.
    B. Marijuana users tend to exhibit problems with concentration and memory.
    C. Synthetic cannabinoids are rarely addictive and do not produce withdrawal effects.
    D. One of the primary consequences of smoking marijuana is a stimulant high that keeps individuals awake all night.

21. Which of the following are used to relieve anxiety and fear?

    A. Steroids
    B. Hypnotics
    C. Opiates
    D. Sedatives

22. Which of the following models is most likely supported by Alcoholics Anonymous?

    A. Moral model
    B. Disease model
    C. Sociological model
    D. Predisposition model

23. Smoking cigars and pipes is closely correlated with a higher risk of

    A. esophageal cancer.
    B. bladder cancer.
    C. pancreatic cancer.
    D. lung cancer.

24. A protein to which neurotransmitters or drugs bind is a(n)

    A. axon.
    B. hormone.
    C. synapse.
    D. receptor.

25. Which of the following is an effect of inhalant usage?

    A. Paranoia
    B. Hallucinations
    C. Manic excitement
    D. Uncoordinated movements

26. A highly potent form of marijuana is

    A. hashish.
    B. opium.
    C. cannabis.
    D. hemp.

27. How soon after a dosage does a heroin addict usually experience the onset of withdrawal symptoms?

    A. 3 hours
    B. 6 hours
    C. 12 hours
    D. 24 hours

28. All of the following factors are used to estimate a person's blood alcohol level EXCEPT:

    A. Alcohol consumption
    B. Gender
    C. Alcohol metabolism
    D. Weight

29. Which of the following is a group of hormones abused by athletes to increase muscle mass?

    A. Amphetamines
    B. Androgens
    C. Creatines
    D. Opiates

30. Which of the following is a stimulant most likely to produce paranoia during use?

    A. Cocaine
    B. Alcohol
    C. Hashish
    D. Ecstasy

31. Which of the following consists of the brain and the spinal cord?

    A. Peripheral nervous system
    B. Central nervous system
    C. Autonomic nervous system
    D. Somatic nervous system

32. Low doses of inhaled aerosols most often cause

    A. dizziness.
    B. suffocation.
    C. sleep.
    D. hypoxia.

33. Where does the majority of alcohol metabolism take place?

    A. Kidneys
    B. Pancreas
    C. Liver
    D. Stomach

34. The idea that drug use behaviors are established by observing family and friends is the

    A. structural influence theory.
    B. cultural trend theory.
    C. social learning theory.
    D. biological theory.

35. All of the following are effects of nicotine EXCEPT:

    A. Increased desire to drink
    B. Decreased oxygen in blood
    C. Increased blood pressure
    D. Decreased desire to eat

36. The inhalation of cigarette smoke in the environment by non-smokers is referred to as

    A. mainstream smoke.
    B. secondhand smoke.
    C. sidestream smoke.
    D. passive smoke.

37. Which of the following is used as a cough suppressant?

    A. Amphetamines
    B. Codeine
    C. Barbiturates
    D. Morphine

38. The loss of sensitivity to the use of a given drug by target cells results in which of the following?

    A. Dependence
    B. Habituation
    C. Reinforcement
    D. Tolerance

39. Which of the following would be considered a gateway drug?

    A. Heroin
    B. Cocaine
    C. LSD
    D. Nicotine

40. The neurotransmitter that is associated with intense euphoria is

    A. norepinephrine.
    B. acetylcholine.
    C. dopamine.
    D. GABA.

41. During which stage of alcohol withdrawal do hallucinations typically first occur?

    A. Stage 1
    B. Stage 2
    C. Stage 3
    D. Stage 4

42. Until the 1800s, the most popular way to use tobacco was by

    A. rubbing it on the gums.
    B. smoking cigarettes.
    C. smoking cigars.
    D. dipping snuff.

43. Which of the following ethnic groups accounts for the lowest percentage of illicit drug use in America?

    A. Asians
    B. Latinos
    C. African Americans
    D. Native Americans

44. Marijuana has been approved for the medical treatment of

    A. glaucoma.
    B. depression.
    C. appetite stimulation in anorexics.
    D. nausea caused by chemotherapy.

45. Which of the following statements best describes amotivational syndrome?

    A. Smoking marijuana produces motivation in smaller doses.
    B. Smoking marijuana creates a lack of motivation in the user.
    C. Smoking marijuana leads to brain damage.
    D. Smoking marijuana creates physical dependence that affects motivation.

46. Which of the following is true of antipsychotic drugs and their effects on schizophrenia?

A. Antipsychotics cure symptoms of schizophrenia.
B. Antipsychotics can often shorten the course of a schizophrenic episode.
C. Atypical antipsychotics have more side effects than other antipsychotics.
D. Atypical antipsychotics take at least one to two weeks to begin to take effect.

47. Which nervous system would be responsible for smelling a flower?

A. Autonomic
B. Central
C. Somatic
D. Involuntary

48. One of the potential side effects related to the medical use of amphetamines is

A. Alzheimer's disease.
B. neuromuscular damage.
C. Parkinson's disease.
D. cardiovascular damage.

49. Which of the following is a colorless, volatile liquid alkaloid that is highly addictive?

A. Nicotine
B. Heroin
C. Alcohol
D. Toluene

50. Which of the following would relieve pain?

A. Amphetamines
B. Cocaine
C. Prozac
D. Opium

51. Which of the following drugs would have the highest potential risk for abuse?

A. Ketamine
B. Ritalin
C. Heroin
D. Ambien

52. Which of the following has the fewest side effects in the treatment of moderate to severe depression?

A. MAOIs
B. Lithium
C. SSRIs
D. Tricyclics

53. Which drug is a member of the barbiturate category and would help an individual sleep?

A. Ambien
B. Phenobarbital
C. Valium
D. Xanax.

54. Which of the following increases the rate at which alcohol is absorbed in the body?

A. Soda
B. Food
C. Water
D. Coffee

55. Side effects of high doses of anabolic steroids may include all of the following EXCEPT:

A. Uncontrolled rage
B. Frequent headaches
C. Visual hallucinations
D. Increased aggression

56. All of the following are associated with employees who abuse alcohol EXCEPT:

   A. Criminal activity
   B. Absenteeism
   C. Accidents
   D. Tardiness

57. Which neurotransmitters are made more available to the brain with antidepressant medication?

   A. Serotonin and dopamine
   B. Acetylcholine and dopamine
   C. Norepinephrine and serotonin
   D. Glutamate and norepinephrine

58. Which of the following is an opioid?

   A. Ritalin
   B. Codeine
   C. Prozac
   D. Ecstasy

59. Which of the following neurotransmitters would provide a sedative effect?

   A. GABA
   B. Acetylcholine
   C. Epinephrine
   D. Norepinephrine

60. Which of the following drugs would be a low risk for potential abuse?

   A. Adderall
   B. Peyote
   C. Fentanyl
   D. Motofen

ANSWER KEY AND EXPLANATIONS

1. D	13. D	25. D	37. B	49. A
2. C	14. C	26. A	38. D	50. D
3. A	15. D	27. B	39. D	51. C
4. D	16. A	28. C	40. C	52. C
5. C	17. C	29. B	41. B	53. B
6. B	18. D	30. A	42. D	54. A
7. B	19. D	31. B	43. A	55. C
8. D	20. B	32. A	44. D	56. A
9. B	21. D	33. C	45. B	57. C
10. C	22. B	34. C	46. B	58. B
11. B	23. A	35. A	47. C	59. A
12. D	24. D	36. D	48. D	60. D

1. **The correct answer is D.** Amphetamines may be prescribed for attention deficit hyperactivity disorder (ADHD), narcolepsy, and obesity. In the past, amphetamines were prescribed for depression (choice A) and asthma, (choice B) but the FDA ended that practice in 1970. Amphetamines were never used in the treatment of epilepsy, so choice C is incorrect.

2. **The correct answer is C.** Distillation is the process of making a concentrated spirit, such as brandy or whiskey, by heating the mixture, collecting the vapors, and condensing the vapors back to a liquid form. Fermentation (choice A) is used to make beer and wine and involves a combination of yeast, sugar, and water but no heat. Inhalation (choice B) is unrelated to the whiskey-making process. Prohibition (choice D) was the period from 1920–1933 when the manufacture and sale of alcohol was illegal in the United States.

3. **The correct answer is A.** The effects of hallucinogens can last up to 12 hours, but rarely beyond that point.

4. **The correct answer is D.** A treatment plan normally lasts 90 days, after which the client and counselor must construct a new plan with new objectives and review what has and has not been accomplished.

5. **The correct answer is C.** One of the side effects of antipsychotic drugs is movement disorders similar to Parkinson's disease. Hand tremors, muscular rigidity, and a shuffling walk occur in about 20 percent of patients taking phenothiazines. Short-term memory loss (choice A), suicidal thoughts (choice B), and depression (choice D) are not common side effects of antipsychotic drugs.

6. **The correct answer is B.** Marijuana has a very low physical dependency level. Methadone has a high physical dependency level, so choice A is incorrect. Both alcohol (choice C) and codeine (choice D) have moderate dependency levels.

7. **The correct answer is B.** Marijuana is the most commonly used illicit drug in the United States. While barbiturates (choice A) and cocaine (choice C) are illicit drugs, they are not used as commonly as marijuana. Alcohol (choice D) is a legal substance abused by many people.

8. **The correct answer is D.** Prescription drugs can be just as dangerous as illicit drugs. The opposite of choice A is true. Barbiturates replaced bromides due to the toxic nature of bromides. The opposite of choice B is true as well. Benzodiazepines do produce withdrawal and dependency effects. Choice C is inaccurate. Most illicit use of anti-anxiety drugs is due to prescription misuse.

9. **The correct answer is B.** According to the moral model, lifestyle choices and immorality are personal choices and therefore are the reason people become drug dependent. Peer pressure (choice A) is a sociological reason for drug dependency. Personality traits (choice C) refers to the personality predisposition model. Biological conditions (choice D) refers to the disease model of dependency.

10. **The correct answer is C.** The temperance movement of the 1800s began as an attempt to encourage moderate drinking of beer and wine when the consumption of hard liquor was associated with criminal activity. The movement later advocated abstinence from all alcohol, so choice A is close but incorrect. Marijuana legalization (choice B) is not related to the temperance movement. Prohibition laws of 1920 outlawed alcohol in the United States and developed out of the temperance movement, so choice D is incorrect.

11. **The correct answer is B.** The neurotransmitter is responsible for carrying messages across the synapse from one neuron to the next. The cell body (choice A) contains the nucleus and resides within the neuron. The dendrites (choice C) receive the transmitted signals. The axon (choice D) is the long part of the cell body.

12. **The correct answer is D.** The only schedule of drugs that can be dispensed without a prescription is Schedule V. Choices A, B, and C represent schedules with stronger restrictions for prescribing medication, and all require a prescription of some sort.

13. **The correct answer is D.** Serotonin includes indole. Norepinephrine (choice A), dopamine (choice B), and epinephrine (choice C) are neurotransmitters that are considered catecholamines.

14. **The correct answer is C.** Nitrous oxide, known as "laughing gas," was first abused in the eighteenth century. People inhaled the substance to achieve a quick state of drunkenness. Ether (choice B) and chloroform (choice D) are two other types of gaseous anesthetics, but they were not used first. Amyl nitrite (choice A) became popular in the 1960s.

15. **The correct answer is D.** Withdrawal symptoms are most associated with drug dependency, which means that a person uses
a drug so frequently that going without it causes physical and
psychological problems. Drug misuse (choice A) refers to using
a prescription drug incorrectly, which is not likely to lead to
withdrawal symptoms. Substance abuse (choice B) may lead to
dependency, but the abuse of alcohol or drugs does not necessarily cause withdrawal symptoms. Psychoactive drugs (choice C)
lead to withdrawal symptoms only if a person becomes dependent
on them.

16. **The correct answer is A.** THC, which is delta-9-tetrahydrocan-
nabinol, is the main active ingredient in marijuana. MDMA
(choice B) is an amphetamine derivative. Cannabis (choice C) is
the plant from which marijuana is derived. Marinol (choice D) is
a synthetic THC prescribed for the treatment of nausea in
cancer patients.

17. **The correct answer is C.** Gender and body weight are less likely
to affect a smoker's risk of cancer. A smoker's risk of cancer
increases with the number of cigarettes smoked on a daily basis,
the number of years spent smoking, and the age when smoking
began.

18. **The correct answer is D.** Bootlegging and black market liquor
sales increased during Prohibition because these were the only
ways to acquire alcohol between 1920 and 1933. Criminal activity
and corruption increased during Prohibition, so choice A is
incorrect. Narcotics usage did not change because of Prohibition,
so choice B is incorrect. Alcohol consumption did not decrease
during Prohibition because people who wanted to drink went to
speakeasies or bootleggers, so choice C is incorrect.

19. **The correct answer is D.** Anhedonia, which is the loss of pleasure, is a short-term effect of cocaine withdrawal. Heavy sweating
(choice A) and seizures (choice C) are associated with alcohol
withdrawal. Heavy smokers lose some sensitivity in their taste
buds, so choice B is incorrect.

20. **The correct answer is B.** Marijuana users tend to exhibit problems with concentration and memory. The high from smoking a marijuana cigarette lasts about 2 to 3 hours, not 6 to 7 hours as choice A erroneously indicates. The opposite of choice C is true. Synthetic cannabinoids are addictive and produce withdrawal effects. Choice D is incorrect because one of the primary consequences of smoking marijuana is the lack of focus and motivation, not a high that keeps individuals up all night.

21. **The correct answer is D.** Sedatives are CNS depressants used to relieve anxiety and fear. Hypnotics (choice B) are also CNS depressants, but they are intended to help people sleep. Steroids and opiates (choices A and C) are not drugs used for the relief of nervousness or anxiety.

22. **The correct answer is B.** Alcoholics Anonymous (AA) and Narcotics Anonymous advocate the disease model, which asserts that people abuse drugs and alcohol because of biological conditions. The moral model (choice A) and the predisposition model (choice D) are two other dependency models that are less likely to be supported by AA. The same with choice C. Sociological theories of drug dependency suggest that social relationships lead to substance abuse.

23. **The correct answer is A.** Cancers of the esophagus, mouth, and larynx are more common among pipe and cigar smokers. Cigarette smoking increases the risk of lung, bladder, pancreas, and kidney cancer.

24. **The correct answer is D.** Receptors are special proteins to which neurotransmitters and drugs bind, which causes the cell function to change. The axon (choice A) is part of the neuron. Hormones (choice B) are chemical messengers released by glands. The synapse (choice C) is the location at which two neurons communicate.

25. **The correct answer is D.** Uncoordinated movements and slurred speech are the typical effects associated with inhalant usage. Inhalants are categorized as depressants because they have similar effects to the use of alcohol and barbiturates. Paranoia and manic excitement (choices A and C) are effects of stimulants, such as cocaine and amphetamines. Hallucinations (choice B) are linked to using hallucinogens, such as Ecstasy and LSD.

26. **The correct answer is A.** Hashish is a potent form of marijuana that contains high levels of THC and may cause hallucinations. Opium (choice B) is not a form of marijuana. Cannabis (choice C) is another name for marijuana. Hemp (choice D) is derived from the wood stem of the cannabis plant and is used to make products such as cloth and rope.

27. **The correct answer is B.** Six hours after a dose, a heroin addict is likely to experience anxiety and cravings, which are the first signs of withdrawal. Most heavy users inject themselves every 4 to 6 hours to avoid the unpleasant effects of withdrawal.

28. **The correct answer is C.** The amount of alcohol consumed and the gender and weight of an individual are factors used to estimate a person's blood alcohol level. Alcohol metabolism refers to the way alcohol is broken down by enzymes in the body. Alcohol metabolism occurs at a constant rate no matter a person's weight or gender.

29. **The correct answer is B.** Androgens are hormones abused by athletes that are found in anabolic steroids. Athletes have used both amphetamines (choice A) and creatine (choice C), but neither one is a hormone. Opiates (choice D) are not hormones.

30. **The correct answer is A.** Cocaine is a stimulant that can cause feelings of paranoia during use. Alcohol (choice B) is a depressant. Hashish (choice C) is a cannabinoid. Ecstasy (choice D) is a hallucinogen.

31. The correct answer is B. The central nervous system consists of the brain and spinal cord and is responsible for learning and memory. The autonomic nervous system (choice C) controls involuntary actions of the body like blood pressure. The somatic nervous system (choice D) controls voluntary actions like chewing. The autonomic and somatic nervous systems together comprise the peripheral nervous system (choice A).

32. The correct answer is A. Dizziness and lightheadedness usually occur with low doses of aerosols such as spray paint. While suffocation (choice B) and hypoxia (choice D) can occur in some cases of inhalation, it usually takes extremely large doses for these to occur. Sleep (choice C) occurs with high doses.

33. The correct answer is C. The liver metabolizes over 90 percent of all alcohol that a person consumes, which is why liver problems occur among heavy drinkers.

34. The correct answer is C. According to the social learning theory, individuals learn drug use behaviors from family and friends. Structural influence theory (choice A) points to the organization of a society or subculture as the greatest influence on an individual's drug use. Cultural trend theory (choice B) is not a drug use behavior theory. Biological theories (choice D) suggest that substance abuse derives from genetics and biological conditions.

35. The correct answer is A. Although smokers may drink alcohol while smoking, there is no indication that nicotine increases the desire to drink. Nicotine increases blood pressure, heart rate, and blood flow. The ability of blood to carry oxygen is decreased by nicotine, and the desire to eat diminishes as well, at least for a short time.

36. The correct answer is D. Passive smoke is the smoke inhaled from the environment by a nonsmoker. Mainstream smoke (choice A) is the smoke a smoker directly takes in when he or she inhales. Secondhand and sidestream smoke (choices B and C) are the same and refer to the smoke that comes off of the lit end of the cigarette.

37. **The correct answer is B.** Codeine is a cough suppressant that is also used for treating moderate pain. Amphetamines (choice A) and barbiturates (choice C) are not used for cough suppression. Morphine (choice D) is another opioid used to relieve pain without inducing sleep.

38. **The correct answer is D.** When target cells lose their sensitivity to a substance, more of the substance is needed to create the same feeling because the body has developed a tolerance for the substance. Dependence (choice A) is the set of physiological consequences exhibited when an individual stops using a substance they have become tolerant to. Habituation (choice B) describes a process in which an individual fails to react to a given external stimulus as forcefully as the stimulus is continuously presented. Reinforcement (choice C) refers to a method of strengthening a given response to a behavior.

39. **The correct answer is D.** Nicotine is considered a gateway drug. Gateway drugs are defined as drugs that have relatively low psychotic effects, such as nicotine or marijuana. Gateway drugs lead to more serious drugs such as heroin (choice A), cocaine (choice B), and LSD (choice C).

40. **The correct answer is C.** Dopamine is associated with mood elevation, and many abused drugs alter the dopamine neurons of the body. Norepinephrine (choice A) is associated with arousal and attentiveness. Acetylcholine (choice B) is linked to mild euphoria, excitability, and insomnia. GABA (choice D), which is linked to alcohol and barbiturates, causes depression and drowsiness.

41. **The correct answer is B.** Hallucinations usually first appear in the second stage of alcohol withdrawal. Stage 1 involves tremors and restlessness, while Stage 3 involves disorientation. Seizures are symptomatic of the fourth stage of alcohol withdrawal.

42. **The correct answer is D.** Dipping snuff, chewing tobacco, and smoking pipes were the most popular methods of using tobacco. Native Americans often made syrup out of tobacco and rubbed it on their gums. Some people enjoyed cigars, but snuff was considered fashionable. Cigarettes did not become popular until the late 1800s, when a cigarette-rolling machine was invented.

43. **The correct answer is A.** Asians have the lowest percentage of illicit drug use, while Native Americans have the highest. Latinos and African Americans are both more frequent users than Asians but less frequent users than Native Americans.

44. **The correct answer is D.** Nausea caused by chemotherapy may be treated with Marinol, a synthetic THC. Marinol may also be given to AIDS patients to help with appetite stimulation, but not to anorexics (choice C). Marijuana may be beneficial to the treatment of patients with glaucoma (choice A) and depression (choice B), but the FDA has not given approval for such use.

45. **The correct answer is B.** The theory behind amotivational syndrome is that smoking marijuana leads to a decrease in motivation. Choices A, C, and D are incorrect.

46. **The correct answer is B.** Antipsychotics do not cure symptoms of schizophrenia, choice A. Atypical antipsychotics have fewer side effects than other antipsychotics (choice C) and can begin easing symptoms as quickly as the first day (choice D).

47. **The correct answer is C.** The somatic nervous system is responsible for voluntary actions, such as smelling a flower. The autonomic nervous system (choice A) is responsible for involuntary actions such as heart rate. The central nervous system (choice B) is responsible for learning and memory. Choice D is not the name of one of the nervous systems.

48. **The correct answer is D.** Cardiovascular damage is a potential side effect of therapeutic amphetamine usage. Amphetamines increase heart rate and blood pressure and may damage veins and arteries. Patients with a history of heart attacks, hypertension, or heart arrhythmia are at an even higher risk of cardiovascular damage. Choices A, B, and C are not side effects known to be associated with amphetamine usage.

49. **The correct answer is A.** Nicotine is a colorless, volatile liquid alkaloid that is highly addictive and found in tobacco. Heroin (choice B) is addictive, but it is not a liquid alkaloid. Alcohol (choice C) is addictive for some people, but not everyone. Toluene (choice D) is a chemical found in glues and paints.

50. **The correct answer is D.** Opium is an opioid. Opioids are used to help manage pain symptoms. Amphetamines (choice A) are stimulants, as is cocaine (choice B). Prozac (choice C) is a psycho-therapeutic drug.

51. **The correct answer is C.** According to the DEA schedule, heroin is classified as a Schedule I drug, which presents the highest risk for substance abuse. Choice B is a Schedule II drug, which carries a lower risk than a Schedule I drug. Choice A is a Schedule III drug, and choice D is a Schedule IV drug.

52. **The correct answer is C.** Selective reuptake inhibitors (SSRIs) are considered the safest antidepressant medication with the fewest side effects. Both tricyclics and MAOIs (Choices D and A) are antidepressant medications, but they both have significant side effects. Lithium (choice B) is a mood stabilizer used for the treat-ment of bipolar patients.

53. **The correct answer is B.** Phenobarbital is a barbiturate that acts to help an individual sleep. Barbiturates have been widely replaced with benzodiazepines, including Ambien, Valium, and Xanax. Choices A, C, and D are incorrect.

54. **The correct answer is A.** Carbonated beverages increase the rate that alcohol is absorbed in the body. Food and water decrease the rate of absorption, so choices B and C are incorrect. Coffee is falsely linked to the metabolism of alcohol, and it does not affect alcohol absorption.

55. **The correct answer is C.** Negative side effects of taking high doses of anabolic steroids include uncontrolled rage, headaches, aggression, anxiety, and insomnia. Visual hallucinations are not known side effects associated with anabolic steroid usage.

56. **The correct answer is A.** Being absent from work or frequently late are typical characteristics of alcoholic employees. Employees who have alcohol or drug abuse issues are also involved in more accidents than employees who do not abuse drugs or alcohol. Therefore, the correct answer is choice A. Unlike individuals who abuse narcotics, most alcoholics are able to support themselves with employment instead of criminal acts.

57. **The correct answer is C.** Antidepressants trigger either nor-epinephrine or serotonin in the brain to help relieve depression symptoms. Dopamine is made more available to the brain by cocaine and causes euphoria and agitation, so choices A and B are incorrect. Glutamate is found throughout the body and is not specifically triggered by antidepressants.

58. **The correct answer is B.** Codeine is an opioid, which is a category of drugs that relieves pain. Ritalin is a stimulant, so choice A is incorrect. Prozac is a psychotherapeutic, so choice C is incorrect. Ecstasy is a hallucinogen, so choice D is incorrect.

59. **The correct answer is A.** GABA is the neurotransmitter that would have a sedative effect in the brain. Choices B, C, and D are incorrect.

60. **The correct answer is D.** Motofen is a Schedule V drug, which is the lowest risk category in the DEA schedule. Choice B is a Schedule I drug, with the highest risk, and choices A and C are Schedule II drugs, with higher risks than a Schedule V drug.

Printed in the USA
CPSIA information can be obtained
at www.ICGtesting.com
JSHW012043140824
68134JS00033B/3226